THE

QUOTABLE

COACH

LEADERSHIP AND MOTIVATION FROM HISTORY'S GREATEST COACHES

BY THOM LOVERRO

CAREER
PRESS

Franklin Lakes, NJ

© 2002 by Thom Loverro

THE QUOTABLE COACH
EDITED BY KRISTEN MOHN
TYPESET BY JOHN J. O'SULLIVAN
Cover design by Design Concept
Printed in the U.S.A. by Book-mart Press

To order this title, please call toll-free 1-800-CAREER-1 (NJ
and Canada: 201-848-0310) to order using VISA or MasterCard,
or for further information on books from Career Press.

The Career Press, Inc.,
3 Tice Road, PO Box 687,
Franklin Lakes, NJ 07417
www.careerpress.com

Library of Congress Cataloging-in-Publication Data

The quotable coach : leadership and motivation from history's greatest coaches /
[compiled] by Thom Loverro.
    p. cm.
  ISBN 1-56414-645-6 (paper)
    1. Sports—Quotations, maxims, etc. 2. Coaching (Athletics)—Quotations,
maxims, etc. 3. Coaches (Athletics)—Quotations. I. Loverro, Thom.

PN6084.S72 Q68 2002
796—dc21   2002031191

DEDICATION

*To the people who have said the words I will carry with
me throughout my life:
my wife, Elizabeth;
my two sons, Rocco and Nick,
and my parents, Andy and Irene.*

CONTENTS

Foreword	7	Cards	71
Introduction	9	Challenges	71
Ability	11	Champions	71
Accomplishments	11	Championships	72
Accountability	11	Character	73
Adversity	12	Cheating	73
Advice	12	Clothes	74
Age	13	Coaching	74
Anthems	13	Commissioners	79
Arrogance	13	Committees	80
Attitude	13	Commitment	80
Authority	14	Communication	80
Awards	14	Competition	81
Sparky Anderson	15	Complaining	82
Red Auerbach	29	Confidence	82
Ballplayers	37	Consistency	82
Baseball	38	Credit	83
Basketball	41	Crime	83
Beauty	42	Criticism	83
Biorhythms	42	Cursing	83
Boss, The	42	Dancing	85
Yogi Berra	43	Death	85
Bobby Bowden	51	Dedication	86
Bear Bryant	61	Defeat	86

Defense	86	
Demons	86	
Desire	87	
Details	87	
Determination	88	
Discipline	89	
Dreams	89	
Drinking	89	
Dynasties	90	
Education	91	
Effort	91	
Emotion	92	
Excellence	92	
Excuses	92	
Experts	92	
Faith	93	
Fans	94	
Fear	96	
Fighting	96	
Flexibility	97	
Food	97	
Football	97	
Friendships	99	
Fundamentals	99	
Eddie Futch	101	
Goals	109	
Greatness	110	
Golf	110	
Hockey	111	
Home field	112	
Home runs	112	
Honesty	112	
Humor	113	
Hustle	113	
Ignorance	115	
Individualists	115	
Injuries	115	
Intelligence	116	
Intensity	118	
Jobs	119	
Bobby Knight	123	
Leadership	135	
Learning	135	
Leisure	135	
Life	136	
Losing	136	
Luck	140	
Tom Landry	141	
Tommy Lasorda	149	
Vince Lombardi	163	
Managing	175	
Marriage	177	
Mistakes	178	
Money	179	
Morale	179	
Motivation	180	
Offense	181	
Olympics	181	
Opening Day	181	
Opportunity	182	
Owners	182	
Passion	183	
People	183	
Performance	184	
Persistence	184	
Perspective	184	
Physique	185	
Pitching	185	
Players	186	
Politics	187	
Popularity	187	
Potential	187	
Practice	188	
Praise	188	

Preparation	189	Sportsmanship	230
Pressure	190	Sportswriters	231
Pride	190	Spouses	231
Problems	190	Stadiums	231
Joe Paterno	191	Statistics	232
Race	201	Strategy	232
Referees	202	Stress	233
Rejection	202	Success	234
Revenge	203	Superstitions	234
Respect	203	Casey Stengel	235
Responsibility	203	Talent	251
Retirement	203	Teaching	255
Rivalries	204	Teams	255
Rules	204	Teamwork	256
Eddie Robinson	205	Temper	258
Frank Robinson	211	Thinking	258
Knute Rockne	219	Ties	258
Sanity	227	Trades	258
Scandal	228	John Thompson	259
Schedules	228	Umpires	269
Selfishness	228	Underachieving	270
Selflessness	229	Uniforms	270
Service	229	Values	271
Sex	229	Winning	273
Sleep	229	Work ethic	276
Smoking	230	John Wooden	277
Soul	230	About the Author	287

FOREWORD

BY

COACH JOHN THOMPSON

The right words, "the use of the right language," are extremely important when you are a coach and you are dealing with a player. It is the art of communication, and like most keys to leadership, it is done through preparation.

Hearing is a physical thing. Listening is psychological, it is based on someone's experience. A player may be hearing me say something else based on his experiences.

You have to know who you are talking to in relation to what you are trying to convey. You have to put yourself in that boy's body and know what he is hearing you say as well as being able to say the right thing.

The preparation for that is done in practice. You prepare that player for when you're speaking to him in the heat of the moment, when you've got to abbreviate what you want to convey and abbreviate it harshly, when the pressure is there. You prepare them to understand how you communicate, which in turn helps with motivation.

Motivation comes from communication. If you are going to motivate somebody, to move a person, which is what coaching is, you have got to be able to communicate. You achieve that through preparation, getting the player used to the way you communicate. If I am trying to motivate a player in a particular situation, and do so loudly and maybe with profanity, it will have a different meaning to a layperson just hearing it than to the player I am trying to motivate. If you have prepared right, that player knows that you care for him and understands what you are trying to accomplish.

Using the right words, "coming up with the right quotes," is different for different situations. You have to have a good read on people, and have to be able to do it very quickly.

The most difficult part of communicating as a coach is talking to the public, not because you seek their seal of approval, but because it is very difficult to be open and honest in an interview as a coach. You infringe on so many privacies involving players. I've got to protect the player and give the public an answer, too. But if the coach is a good coach, he will take the hit. You have a public responsibility to satisfy as a coach, but you don't want to crush somebody or publicly humiliate him. As a college coach, you are still in the role of a teacher and developer of young people. The coaches who I have respect for took a lot of hits for their players and guard what they say, speaking publicly in a certain way.

It truly is an art, the ability to communicate, particularly in a situation where you are going to be quoted. It is hard to get messages across sometimes without being misunderstood. But it's expected of you, as a coach, to find the right thing to say at the right time.

—*John Thompson is a member of the Basketball Hall of Fame for his accomplishments as a basketball coach at Georgetown University, where he compiled a record of 596-239, with three NCAA Final Four appearances and one National Championship in 1984. He is currently a television analyst for NBA basketball and host of a Washington, D.C. radio talk show.*

INTRODUCTION

I n sports, coaches get paid big bucks to talk to some of the biggest business executives in the United States, and it's not about moving a player into the low post, or running the triangle offense, or pass patterns, or the value of the hit-and-run play. They pay that big money to hear what coaches say about winning, life, and anything else they can carry away with them to use in creating their own success.

People want to capture the mystique that surrounds what motivates grown men and women to suffer insults and indignities to become winners. They want the words that move these athletes to pursue excellence.

Coaches have to learn the art of communication in a very particular way: short, inspirational phrases that crystallize the concepts of motivation and determination. They have to communicate to their players what it takes to win.

In our modern world of communication, they might be called sound bites. But they are quotes, first and foremost, and sports coaches, perhaps more than any other professional in the U.S., are the best at delivering them. After all, it wasn't Vince Lombardi's coaching skills that made his players admire him despite his tough treatment (one Green Bay Packer once said of Lombardi, "He treats all of us the same—like dogs"). It was his tough words.

The coach who is quotable does not always just fit in the category of winning, losing, or any other categories that seem like life and death. Coaches also often have a good sense of humor, and can laugh through difficult moments, or simply get his or her message across with some wit. They often have observations, about some of the greatest athletes who have ever taken the field of play, that no one else could have come up with, and also have a perspective on the trials and tribulations of winning and losing that most of us never experience.

Words to stoke your competitive fires, touch your heart, or make you laugh—coaches, as much as anyone, use those words, and provide a wealth of inspiration, insight, and fun.

They are experts in the sports where they have risen to the level of coach, but they are more than that. They are storytellers and observers of the human experience, which is all part of being a quotable coach.

ABILITY

"I won't accept anything less than the best a player's capable of doing...and he has the right to expect the best that I can do for him and the team."

—Football coach Lou Holtz

ACCOMPLISHMENTS

"My boy, one small breeze doesn't make a wind storm."

—New York Giants manager John McGraw

"If what you have done yesterday still looks big to you. You haven't done much today."

—Duke basketball coach Mike Krzyzewski

ACCOUNTABILITY

"I learned early that if I wanted to achieve anything in life, I'd have to do it myself. I learned that I had to be accountable."

—Basketball coach Lenny Wilkens

ADVERSITY

"Even in the most impossible situations, stand tall, keep our heads up, shoulders back, keep moving, running, looking up, demonstrating our pride, dignity, and defiance."

—Football coach Bill Walsh

"In adversity there is opportunity."

—Football coach Lou Holtz

"Know how to win and how to lose and be able to handle adversity."

—Nebraska football coach Tom Osborne

"Adversity is an opportunity for heroism."

—Football coach Marv Levy

"When you're playing against a stacked deck, compete even harder. Show the world how much you'll fight for the winner's circle. If you do, someday the cellophane will crackle off a fresh pack, one that belongs to you, and the cards will be stacked in your favor."

—Basketball coach Pat Riley

ADVICE

"Get in front of those balls, you won't get hurt. That's what you've got a chest for, young man."

*—New York Giants manager John McGraw
offering fielding advice to Heinie Groh*

"To be a good hitter you've got to do one thing: get a good ball to hit."

—Manager Roger Hornsby

Age

"I've been here so long that when I got here the Dead Sea wasn't even sick."

—*Alabama basketball coach Wimp Sanderson*

"I may go on forever, because statistics say that few men die after the age of 100."

—*Football coach Amos Alonzo Stagg on his 100th birthday*

"There are three ages: youth, adult, and 'Hey, you're looking good.'"

—*Track coach Leroy Walker*

Anthems

"We're going to be the best in the league at something. We're deep in anthem singers."

—*Nashville Predators hockey coach Barry Trotz*

Arrogance

"I'm too arrogant and too competitive to think we won't win this year. Really, I find the situation we're in energizing. What should I do, crawl into the fetal position and just lay there? All I know is this: Any time I want to, I can open this little case in my house, look at my Super Bowl ring, and realize I'm not the dumb ass everyone thinks I am."

—*Football coach Brian Billick on his Ravens, who lost 11 of 22 starters from 2001, mostly because of cap reasons*

Attitude

"I told him, 'Son, what is it with you? Is it ignorance or apathy?' He said, 'Coach, I don't know, and I don't care.'"

—*NBA coach Frank Layden, commenting on the attitude of one of his players*

"Ability is what you're capable of doing. Motivation determines what you do. Attitude determines how well you do it."

—Football coach Lou Holtz

"Look at misfortune the same way you look at success: Don't Panic! Do you best and forget the consequences."

—Los Angeles Dodgers manager Walt Alston

"There are positive and negative thoughts. And, hey, it doesn't cost you a cent more to think positively."

—Boxing trainer Angelo Dundee

"It's better to decide wrongly than weakly. If you're weak, you're likely to be wrong anyway."

—Football coach Bill Parcells

"We control by attitudes—positive mental attitudes—not by rules."

—Football coach Woody Hayes

"Great effort springs naturally from great attitude."

—Basketball coach Pat Riley

AUTHORITY

"I'm the only chief. All the rest are Indians."

—Baseball manager Dick Williams

AWARDS

"I don't feel that I deserve this great award, but it makes up for all the years I should have won and didn't."

—Delaware football coach Tubby Raymond
after winning Coach of the Year honors

National Baseball Hall of Fame Library
Cooperstown, N.Y.

SPARKY ANDERSON

G eorge Lee Anderson (later known as Sparky) was born on February 22, 1934, in Bridgewater, South Dakota. He grew up as many midwestern young men did, playing baseball, and dreaming of one day being a major league ballplayer.

A standout second baseman, Anderson would realize that dream. He was signed by the Brooklyn Dodgers and spent six seasons in their farm system before being traded to the Philadelphia Phillies. Anderson made the Phillies major league roster in 1959, but hit a disappointing .218 for the last place club, and that would be the end of Anderson's major league playing days.

Anderson spent the next four seasons back in the minor leagues before moving from the field to the dugout as manager of the Class AAA Toronto Maple Leafs baseball team, at the time owned by a young Jack Kent Cooke. Anderson spent four seasons managing in Toronto before getting the call to the major leagues again—this time as a coach. He was a coach for the San Diego Padres in 1969 and had already taken another coaching job with the California Angels in 1970. However, an opportunity came up that would change Anderson's life: he was hired to manage the Cincinnati Reds.

The Reds were a team on the verge of greatness, with tremendous talent such as catcher Johnny Bench and Pete Rose, and Anderson was the right man to lead them. In his first season in Cincinnati, the Reds won 70 of their first 100 games, the National League West division title and the National League pennant. They would go on to lose to the Baltimore Orioles in the World Series, but the stage was set for the Reds to become the team of the decade, and Anderson, the manager of the decade.

In nine seasons with the Reds, Anderson achieved the highest win total (863) and best winning percentage (.596), of any manager in the history of the franchise. They averaged 96 wins per season, won five divisional titles, four pennants, and two World Championships in 1975 and 1976, with a team referred to as "The Big Red Machine."

Remarkably, the Reds fired Anderson after the 1978 season—the second consecutive year the Reds had finished second. He protested the termination of several coaches, so Anderson was terminated as well.

The Reds never truly recovered from that move, but Anderson did. He was hired to manage the Detroit Tigers, and became the winningest manager in Tigers history, winning two division titles, one pennant, and the 1984 World Series. When he retired after the 1995 season, Anderson had set franchise records for most seasons (17), games (2,579), and wins (1,331) by a manager.

Anderson left behind a winning legacy that put him among the elite managers of the game. He was named Manager of the Year twice in both the National League and the American League. Anderson won more than 600 games in each league and was also the first to win World Championships in both leagues. In all, Anderson had a managing record of 2,194–1,834, and accomplished that with a great baseball mind, a terrific ability to handle great ballplayers, and a great outlook on life.

SPARKY ANDERSON ON:

ACCESSORIES

"Me carrying a briefcase is like a hotdog wearing earrings."

ATTITUDE

"Everyone is special and everyone forgets how fortunate they are. I know how fortunate I've been and that will never be forgotten."

BASEBALL

"Babe Ruth is dead and buried in Baltimore, but the game is bigger and better than ever."

"Baseball is a simple game. If you have good players and if you keep them in the right frame of mind, then the manager is a success."

"The great thing about baseball is when you're done, you'll only tell your grandchildren the good things. If they ask me about 1989, I'll tell them I had amnesia."

"Playing the sport is like having a license to steal. It's like going to the bank with a water pistol...then after you get all the bank's money, you give your address, phone number, and name and tell her to give it to the police...and they'd never come."

COMMISSIONERS

"If I hear Bowie Kuhn say just once more he's doing something for the betterment of baseball, I'm going to throw up."

DESIRE

"The trick is to realize that after giving your best, there's nothing more to give."

EDUCATION

"I only had a high school education and believe me, I had to cheat to get that."

FANS

"It's a terrible thing to have to tell your fans, who have waited like Detroit's have, that their team won't win it this year. But it's better than lying to them."

"I understand people who boo us. It's like going to a Broadway show: you pay for your tickets and expect to be entertained. When you're not, you have a right to complain."

Fate

"You give us the pitching some of these clubs have and no one could touch us, but God has a way of not arranging that, because it's not as much fun."

Future

"People who live in the past generally are afraid to compete in the present. I've got my faults, but living in the past is not one of them. There's no future in it."

Life

"Life is precious. You should make everyone you meet or see happy."

Losing

"I cannot get rid of the hurt from losing, but after the last out of every loss, I must accept that there will be a tomorrow. In fact, it's more than there'll be a tomorrow, it's that I want there to be a tomorrow. That's the big difference, I want tomorrow to come."

Managers

"A baseball manager is a necessary evil."

"I don't believe a manager ever won a pennant. Casey Stengel won all those pennants with the Yankees. How many did he win with the Boston Braves and Mets?"

"My idea of managing is giving the ball to Tom Seaver and sitting down and watching him work."

MONEY

"Just give me 25 guys on the last year of their contracts. I'll win a pennant every year."

PEOPLE

"I can deal with anyone on any side of the track. You have to deal with everyone."

PITCHING

"If I ever find a pitcher who has heat, a good curve, and a slider, I might seriously consider marrying him, or at least proposing."

PLAYERS

"Players have two things to do. Play and keep their mouths shut."

"The only thing I believe is this: A player does not have to like a manager and he does not have to respect a manager. All he has to do is obey the rules."

"The players make the manager, it's never the other way."

RELIGION

"If God let you hit a home run last time up, then who struck you out the time before that?"

TALENT

"If you have to choose between power and speed and it often turns out you have to make that choice, you've got to go for speed."

"The day I got a hit off [Sandy] Koufax was when he knew it was all over."

"I don't want to embarrass any other catcher by comparing him to Johnny Bench."

"The man I marvel at is the one that's in there day after day and night after night, and still puts the figures on the board. I'm talking about Pete Rose, Stan Musial, the real stars. Believe me, especially the way we travel today, flying all night with a game the next night and then the next afternoon, if you can play 162 games, you're a man."

WINNING

"They say the first World Series is the one you remember most. No, no, no. I guarantee you don't remember that one because the fantasy world you always dreamed about is suddenly real."

WORK

"The only reason I'm coming out here tomorrow is the schedule says I have to."

"This game has taken a lot of guys over the years who would have had to work in factories and gas stations and made them prominent people. There isn't a college in the world that would have me and yet in this business you can walk into a room with millionaires, doctors, professional people, and get more attention than they get. I don't know any other business where you can do that."

•••

Sparky Anderson was inducted into the National Baseball Hall of Fame on July 23, 2000. Here is what he had to say on that important day about baseball and life:

"Please sit down. I learned a long time ago at ballparks, when they stand up, they're getting ready to boo. So please, just set it on down.

"First of all, I cannot thank Commissioner Selig, and I thank him so much for introducing me. Because of all the hours we spent together talking, over the years when I went into Milwaukee, and I thank him for his kindness. But he has to be, and he's told me to call him Bud. I could never call him Bud. He is the commissioner. And let me tell all of you this: Whether commissioners sometimes make mistakes, they're human beings. But nobody loves the game of baseball more than this commissioner. He truly loves the game. And when I look out here today. If you don't think baseball is the greatest game that the kids ever made—and the kids have played on the sandlots in the streets of New York as Willie played stickball when he was in the big leagues—if you don't think it's the greatest game, leave, 'cause you're missing it all. It's the greatest game there ever was. It is the only game where nobody cares where you come from. And nobody cares who you are. They only care, can you play. That's all this game is. It's a game of having fun.

"I want all of you at this moment—and it's a must for me, 'cause this will be the last time I ever get to speak, 'cause when I walk away from here today, I'll never win another game, and I'll never lose another game, and I know that; so in that respect it's a sad moment for me, knowing I will never get to get up in front of a group—but, I want you to take a look at the people behind me and put it in your brain, when you look at 'em. The people that came before them, and these people, and the people that will come after them. That is baseball. All the other stuff you've heard about baseball is just a makeup. Those people made this game, and they will protect this game. And when you sit in a room with them, and you look around, you say to yourself, 'My goodness, George Sugar, how could we come from the streets of Santa Barbara to Cincinnati, Ohio? That's impossible. How could a young man from Bridgewater, South Dakota, 600 people, and couldn't play ever be in front of a microphone, and they're talking about the third winningest manager?'

"Well let me tell you this, and get it straight, and I hope every manager that follows me will listen very carefully: Players earn this, by their skills. Managers come here, as I did, on their backs, for what they did for me. I never believed different, I will never believe different, and I think that's what made my career so lucky. I was smart enough to know the people that were doing the work, and I could never under any circumstances ever thank 'em.

"I thank the Veterans' Committee for giving me this honor. I thank Dale Petroskey, and all the people at the Hall of Fame. I wish all of you out there could have had the opportunity I had the last four days. I have never in my lifetime been treated like that. I even told my wife, I said, 'You know they're treating me so good I feel like I'm important. Maybe I'll start acting like I'm important.' She said, 'It wouldn't do no good, cause nobody'd pay any attention.' So you know, that is the way they treat you. And I thank Dale so much. I can't thank you enough.

"I thank the media, and the fans. The fans were very patient with me all the time. Very patient. But the most important thing was the media, 'cause they used to come into my office, and they wore high boots that were up to here. And I got the message, I got the message well. But they thought I was throwing some stuff that wasn't too correct. And they were right. I was throwing a lot of it out there because things weren't going too good, and when things weren't going too good I always learned one thing. Just throw a lot of bologna and keep 'em off track.

"I'm not gonna mention players individually or coaches individually. But I'll tell you this: No coach ever worked for me in my whole career. I worked with coaches, and that was the thing I think I enjoyed so much. We were together. We worked together. They told me many times what to do and I listened. 'Cause you know something? It's a funny thing. There are other people besides the manager that are smart. You know, a manager has that above his door. He can be the dumbest moron there ever was, but as long as he's manager he's got 'Manager' above his door. That don't work.

"There's two kind of managers. One that ain't very smart. He gets bad players, loses games, and gets fired. Then there was somebody like me that was a genius. I got good players, stayed out of the way, let 'em win a lot, and then just hung around for 26 years. It was a lot of fun.

"My family, my family. She will kill me, because my wife does not ever want anything said about her. She don't want to be photographed. She don't want to be interviewed. She let me have all the freedom in the world. And that's the reason I was able to be so lucky. She let me go and let me be free, and that I can never thank her enough for. My wife Carol. She raised my three children, and I cannot take any credit for them being raised. I can take credit now because I can give things. But I can't take nothing for the times that were tough, and she had to raise 'em, and what a job she did. I have three kids today: 42, 39 (and they don't like those ages), 38. But they are the finest young people for me, for me, in this whole world. And that's because of what Carol did.

"First of all I want to introduce my son, Lee, and his wife, Dawn. And then I have my daughter, Shirley. And I always called her Sissy, she thinks I'm nuts, and her husband, Jan. And then the youngest one, Albert, and his wife, Sara. And then all the grandchildren that are here. We have 14, so we won't go into all that. I just want them to know that they have tremendous parents and if they will listen to 'em, they will grow up to be good citizens. And I want them to grow up, for what my father said, when I was 11 years old. My father never got past the third grade, but there ain't a guy that ever went to Harvard smart as my daddy. My daddy said this. He said, 'I'm gonna give you a gift. It's the greatest gift to take all the way through your life. And if you live with this gift, everything will work perfect.' And he said, 'Son, I'm gonna give you a gift that will never cost a dime, and that gift is this: If every day of your life, and every person you meet, you will just be nice to that person, and treat that person like they are someone.' And, you know, I can tell you this. I have tried as hard as I could, and there's no way you can try any harder than I have. My daddy was all man. He didn't need no big degrees to walk tall. He could walk tall just from the way he handled himself.

"Then I would like to tell all my friends, every friend I've ever met, and I've met a lot of 'em: I thank you for everything. I thank everybody up at Sunset Golf Course in Thousand Oaks, because they ain't getting none of my money all this week. I'm the sucker up there and they get all the money. They ain't getting nothing this week.

"I want to thank the 1951 American Legion team I played on in Detroit, Michigan. Won the National Championship. That was right after Frank Robinson killed us in '50—came down from Oakland. And in 1951 we won. And they're here today, a whole bunch of 'em, and I thank you so much.

"I want to thank the 1948 Trojans, the National Champions, that beat Mr. George Bush. We beat 'em two to one, and I was the batboy at USC for six years. And I think that saved my life from the neighborhood I came from. I came from a neighborhood—when you talk about things that are not too good, it wasn't too good. But I tell you what, I wouldn't trade it for one single second. That's what made me, I think, who I am today, is because I came from a neighborhood of good people.

"I want to thank—and I have to so much—for my father, he started me in the game, Rod Dedeaux. I could never tell you about Rod Dedeaux, and I'm not gonna go into it up here. Rod Dedeaux was there and will always be there 'til they put me away. He was like my second daddy. He called my Georgie, and the only other person that did that was my mama. She called me Georgie, Rod Dedeaux called me Georgie.

"Lefty Phillips. If you could only have known Lefty Phillips. Oh, my goodness, what a tremendous man. And this is his day, that I like to think that he's here. And I know he is here in me. I don't know where else, but he's here. Benny Lefebvre, Jimmy Lefebvre's Daddy, my American Legion coach. Bud Brubaker, my high school coach. And Art Mazmanian, who's not here, he coached at Mount Sac for must be 2,000 years he's been at Mount Sac, and he just retired. And George Sugar, my first manager I ever had. And I'll tell you this: He had all the smarts, I had the title. And Georgie, I can never tell you enough what it meant to have you there, 'cause you took care of everything when the problems got tough. And I had a tight one—and the players know what that means—a tight one all the time and Georgie took care of things.

"A man named George Kissell, the greatest single instructor I ever seen on fundamentals in my life. Fifty-some years with the Cardinals. And Georgie—he was something special to me. And then—I'm gonna get it going here—Chief Bender. Goodness Chief, my first farm director, put up with me for 13 years. Had to scream a lot on the phone at me a lot of times 'cause he really didn't like all the things I was doing, but we're tremendous friends. And Dick Wagner. Dick Wagner was my friend when I was at Cincinnati, he's my friend now, and he'll be my friend when I leave this great world of ours.

"Bob Howsam. He's the man who caused me all the trouble. But everybody said why do I wear a Cincinnati hat, why don't I why a Detroit hat? I had no choice. Bob Howsam gave me a job at the age 35 years old. I thought he was crazy. I think the world thought he was crazy. But he had the courage and the vision to see what he wanted to see from a manager. I will always be indebted to him for everything, because everything in my home, everything I put on me, all comes because of this single man, Bob Howsam, hiring me. And I thank you so much Bob.

"And then there's Jim Campbell over at Detroit. James Arthur Campbell. Don't ever forget that name. James Arthur Campbell was so much fun you would go crazy being around him. And I drove him nuts. He said that he was afraid to pick up the paper every morning 'cause he was afraid to see what I was gonna say. I said, 'Jim, don't worry. Cancel your subscription, it'll be no problem.' But, I know he's here today, because I've never forgot him, and I never will forget him.

"And then I'm gonna tell you something special. Dan Ewald. I've known Dan Ewald for 22 years. And me and Dan are like as close as you can possibly get. You couldn't get any closer than we are. And I want Dan to know on this day, he means so much to me.

"And the last, but not least, is my mom and daddy. They're here today. Mama was so quiet and so gentle. She used to say to me, 'Georgie, how come I raised all chiefs and no Indians?' And I said, 'Mama, I don't know why.' But I know this: my mama was a real mama and I enjoyed so much her times.

"I thank all of you and I want you to know that my family and my two sisters who couldn't come are at home. And my brother who couldn't come, and my brother and sister-in-law who couldn't come, and every other person. Don't ever forget how special that is, and don't ever forget as long as you live, you will never in your lifetime see people of that greatness again. Thank you so much."

Steve Lipofsky

RED
AUERBACH

W hen you come up with a short list of all-time winning coaches in the history of sports, Red Auerbach is always on that list. The cigar-smoking basketball guru led the Celtics to nine National Basketball Association championships as a coach, and did so with an outspoken style that made him one of the most quotable coaches in basketball history.

Arnold "Red" Auerbach was born on September 20, 1917 in Brooklyn, N.Y. He played basketball at P.S. 122 in Brooklyn and Eastern District High School. After a year at Seth Low Junior College, Auerbach transferred to George Washington University, where he was a standout basketball player in 1941. He began his coaching career at St. Albans Prep School and Roosevelt High School in Washington, D.C., before serving in the U.S. Navy from 1943 to 1946.

When he came out of the Navy after the war, Auerbach returned to Washington to resume his coaching career—this time on the professional level. He coached the Washington Capitals of the Basketball Association of America to a 49-11 mark, the best record in the league for the 1946–47 season. He left to coach the Tri-Cities Blackhawks for the 1949–50 season, and then, when Celtics owner Walter Brown needed a coach, he hired Auerbach, who used his team concept to build one of the greatest dynasties ever witnessed in sports.

Auerbach began with Bob Cousy as the playmaker for Boston, but it was the trade he made in 1956 that put the Celtics over the top. Auerbach traded center Ed Maccauley and the rights to former Kentucky player Cliff Hagan to the St. Louis Hawks for the rights to draft a star center out of the University of San Francisco, Bill Russell, who immediately paid dividends by leading Boston to its first NBA championship in his rookie year. The Celtics would not repeat, losing to the Hawks in the 1958 finals when Russell was injured, but then Auerbach began his legendary championship run of eight consecutive NBA titles, the last one coming in 1966 against the Los Angeles Lakers.

Even though Auerbach retired from coaching in 1966, he was still the driving force behind the Celtics franchise as general manager and other front office positions, and engineered the titles they won while he was in the front office (another seven NBA titles). He was elected to the Basketball Hall of Fame in 1968, with a coaching record of 1,037 wins against 548 defeats. He coached or drafted some of the greatest players in the history of the game—Russell and Larry Bird among them. He also was a leader in the breaking down of racial barriers in the NBA. In 1950, he became the first to draft an African-American: Chuck Cooper. He was first to start five black players and first to hire a black coach (Russell) in the NBA. He also hired two other black coaches—Satch Sanders and K.C. Jones—both former players of his in Boston. But most of all, he won in style, and spoke in style as well.

Red Auerbach on:

Ability

"Natural abilities are like natural plants: they need pruning by study."

Achievement

"Just do what you do best."

Action

"The only correct actions are those that demand no explanation and no apology."

Attitude

"If you want to be a champion, you've got to feel like one, you've got to act like one, you've got to look like one."

Authority

"The coach should be the absolute boss, but he still should maintain an open mind."

"Don't be so domineering that you want to show and prove that you're the boss every day. Do your job. But listen to people."

"He has the players too happy."

—Criticism of Bill Russell when he was coaching the Celtics in 1966

BASKETBALL

"I look at teams and they have four or five coaches. Maybe I'm old-fashioned, but what do you need them for? You only have five players on the team! The game hasn't changed that much."

"Basketball is like war in that offensive weapons are developed first, and it always takes a while for the defense to catch up."

CHAMPIONSHIPS

"When it was over, I was emotionally spent. I sat alone in the room and said, 'God, isn't this a great feeling, being the coach of the greatest basketball team in the world?'"

> —*Talking about his reaction after winning his first championship with the Celtics in 1957*

"What are they going to do with all of those balloons now? Anybody want to buy some balloons cheap?"

> —*Referring to the balloons ready to be launched in the rafters of the Los Angeles Forum after the Celtics won the 1969 NBA championship there*

CIGARS

"It all boils down to this. I used to hate these college coaches or any coach that was 25 points ahead with three minutes left to go, and they're up there yellin' and coachin' because they're on TV, and they want their picture on, and they get recognition. To me the game was over. The day's work is done. Worry about the next game. This game is over. So I would light a cigar and sit on the bench and just watch it.

The game was over, for all intents and purposes. I didn't want to rub anything in or show anybody what a great coach I was when I was 25 points ahead. Why? I gotta win by 30? What the hell difference does it make? The commissioner [Maurice Podoloff] said you can't smoke the cigars on the bench. But there were guys smoking cigarettes on the bench. I said, 'What is this, an airplane—you can smoke cigarettes but not cigars?' No way. I wouldn't do it.

"I started with a pipe. The pipe was less expensive to start with. The change to a cigar was fortuitous; a 'victory pipe' might not have worked."

"You can't smoke in here! It says so on the menu!"

—A woman sitting in the restaurant Legal Seafood in Boston admonishing Auerbach lighting up a cigar

"No cigar smoking in here...except for Red Auerbach."

—The notice on the menu at Legal Seafood that Auerbach pointed out to the woman

COMPETITION

"You don't kiss your enemy. You see, theoretically, if I'm playing against you, if you make me look bad and I get fired, you're my enemy. That means you're taking the food out of my mouth, out of my family's mouth. So as long as you're my enemy, let's be enemies."

COMMUNICATION

"In any good coach is the ability to communicate. In other words, a lot of coaches know their Xs and Os, but the players must absorb it."

DEDICATION

"Many, many times, the kids with the less talent become the better athletes because they're more dedicated to achieving their full potential."

FANS

"I don't sit in the [luxury] boxes with all that food and all that stuff in there...I like to hear what the people say, even at my age. I like to see if there's any bitching and moaning during the games."

FORGIVENESS

"The best way to forget one's self is to look at the world with attention and love."

INTEGRITY

"To be a successful coach you should be and look prepared. You must be a man of integrity. Never break your word. Don't have two sets of standards. Remember you don't handle players—you handle pets. You deal with players. Stand up for your players. Show them you care—on and off the court. Very important—it's not 'how' or 'what' you say, but what they absorb."

LOGIC

"If you give a guy three points for a long shot, then you should give him just one point for a lay-up."

LOSING

"Show me a good loser, and I'll show you a loser."

Music

"Music washes away from the soul the dust of everyday life."

Performance

"An acre of performance is worth a whole world of promise."

Players

"When I coached, we had some great, great players who could be All-Stars today, from Bill Russell to Wilt Chamberlain to Bob Cousy to Oscar Robertson."

Rivalries

"The Lakers used to complain how hot it was at the Garden, that it wasn't air-conditioned. I said to them, 'Hey, I don't blame you for complaining, because the half-a-court we play on is air-conditioned.' I mean, how f---ing stupid can you be? It was the same for us."

Talent

"I knew right from the beginning that he was headed for the pile. I respect him, he's a helluva coach, he really is...but he didn't like Rick Fox! He didn't like [David] Wesley. He didn't like [Danny] Fortson. You know what I mean...we differed on a lot of things."

—Referring to Rick Pitino's tenure as coach
and general manager of the Boston Celtics

TEAMWORK

"They said you have to use your five best players, but I found you win with the five who fit together the best."

"Team was important. We didn't care who the starting five was."

TRAGEDY

"The bad break of it all was that the league never gave us a chance to recover from Reggie Lewis. Forget about Bias— they never gave us a pick or anything to recover from that— but they could have given us [cap] money to use for Reggie. They made us carry his salary on our cap for three years. Three! Today, they changed [that rule]. They realized how shabbily they treated us."

> —*Referring to the untimely death of Reggie Lewis from a heart ailment and also the death of their number one draft choice in 1986, Maryland star Len Bias, from a cocaine overdose*

WORK ETHIC

"Take a Larry Bird. He worked unbelievably hard. Kevin McHale, Magic Johnson and Michael Jordan would do the same thing. Guys like that loved the game so much, they didn't mind practices. They had a great time. The great players continue to be great, and they want to get better."

BALLPLAYERS

"How to use your leisure time is the biggest problem of a ballplayer."

—Baseball manager and general manager Branch Rickey

"One percent of ballplayers are leaders of men. The other 99 percent are followers of women."

—New York Giants manager John McGraw

"I guess more players lick themselves than are ever licked by an opposing team. The first thing any man has to know is how to handle himself."

—Philadelphia Athletics owner and manager Connie Mack

"You think the greatest thing in the whole world would be to become a baseball player—if best things already happened, what's next?"

—New York Giants manager John McGraw

Eighty percent of big league ballplayers go out to the race-track today. Sneak around in sunglasses. Other 20 percent ain't that holy. Just can't find anybody who'll give 'em free tickets."

—Manager Roger Hornsby

"Any ballplayer that don't sign autographs for little kids ain't an American. He's a communist."

—Manager Roger Hornsby
on ballplayers refusing to sign autographs

"Players who stand flat footed and swing with their arms are golfers, not hitters."

—Manager Roger Hornsby
on the hitting style of ballplayers

"Today's players are only going to do what makes them more money. The agent tells his player what management is looking for and what his player is noted for. Most times it's not for hitting triples. You're either a singles hitter, a doubles hitter, or a home-run hitter. You never hear anyone say, 'That guy's a triples hitter.' I don't know of too many arbitration cases that have been won because the guy could hit triples."

—Kansas City Royals Manager Tony Muser on the
mercenary attitudes of today's baseball players

"A great ballplayer is a player who will take a chance."

—Baseball manager and general manager Branch Rickey

BASEBALL

"Baseball is like church. Many attend, but few understand."

—New York Mets manager Wes Westrum

"There is but one game and that game is baseball."

—*New York Giants manager John McGraw*

"People ask me what I do in winter when there's no baseball. I'll tell you what I do. I stare out the window and wait for spring."

—*Baseball manager Roger Hornsby*

"The key to winning baseball games is pitching, fundamentals, and three-run homers."

—*Baseball manager Earl Weaver*

"There are surprisingly few real students of the game in baseball; partly because everybody, my 83-year-old grandmother included, thinks they learned all there was to know about it at puberty. Baseball is very beguiling that way."

—*Baseball manager Alvin Dark*

"Baseball is a game of inches."

—*Baseball manager and general manager Branch Rickey*

"You can't sit on a lead and run a few plays into the line and just kill the clock. You've got to throw the ball over the damn plate and give the other man his chance. That's why baseball is the greatest game of them all."

—*Baseball manager Earl Weaver*

"There are only five things you can do in baseball: run, throw, catch, hit, and hit with power."

—*Baseball manager Leo Durocher*

"Baseball has been good to me since I quit trying to play it."

—*Manager Whitey Herzog*

"No matter what I talk about, I always get back to baseball."

—Philadelphia Athletics owner
and manager Connie Mack

"Baseball is a kid's game that grownups only tend to screw up."

—Baseball manager Bob Lemon

"The game has kept faith with the public, maintaining its old admission price for nearly 30 years while other forms of entertainment have doubled and tripled in price. And it will probably never change."

—Philadelphia Athletics owner
and manager Connie Mack

"In this game of baseball, you live by the sword and die by it. You hit and get hit. Remember that."

—Baseball manager Alvin Dark

"Man may penetrate the outer reaches of the universe, he may solve the very secret of eternity itself, but for me, the ultimate human experience is to witness the flawless execution of a hit-and-run."

—Baseball manager and general manager Branch Rickey

"The first rule of baseball is to get a good ball to hit."

—Baseball manager Roger Hornsby

"Any minute, any day, some players may break a long-standing record. That's one of the fascinations about the game, the unexpected surprises."

—Philadelphia Athletics owner
and manager Connie Mack

"I don't sit there and watch the clock. That's what's great about baseball. There's no time limit. You can be 25,000 runs behind, but you can keep hitting."

—Baseball manager Johnny Oates after his Texas Ranger played a four-hour-and-21 minute nine-inning game against the Cleveland Indians

"Baseball and malaria keep coming back."

—Baseball manager Gene Mauch

"Every player should be accorded the privilege of at least one season with the Chicago Cubs. That's baseball as it should be played: in God's own sunshine. And that's really living."

—Baseball manager Alvin Dark on the joys of playing day baseball at Wrigley Field—before lights were installed

"Baseball is made up of very few big and dramatic moments, but rather it's a beautifully put together pattern of countless little subtleties that finally add up to the big moment, and you have to be well-versed in the game to truly appreciate them."

—Baseball manager Paul Richards

"This ain't a football game, we do this every day."

—Baseball manager Earl Weaver

BASKETBALL

"Basketball is sharing."

—Basketball coach Phil Jackson

BEAUTY

"Buy one and send it to my mother. It's her fault I look like this."

—*Baseball manager Don Zimmer talking about a
newspaper photo of himself*

BIORHYTHMS

"I think the National League has better biorhythms in July."

—*Baseball manager Earl Weaver on the National League
dominance of the mid-season All-Star Game*

THE BOSS

"Sometimes I would do just the opposite of what George wanted me to do, because I won't let anyone tell me how to manage. If I'm going down the tube, I'm going to do it my way."

—*Baseball manager Billy Martin, on his defiant style
of managing for New York Yankees owner
George Steinbrenner*

"The two of them deserve each other. One's a born liar, the other's convicted."

—*Baseball manager Billy Martin's comparison of
New York Yankees owner George Steinbrenner
and Martin's combative slugger, Reggie Jackson*

"What does George know about Yankee pride? When did he ever play for the Yankees?"

—*Baseball manager Billy Martin, on George
Steinbrenner's lack of connection with Yankee history*

National Baseball Hall of Fame Library
Cooperstown, N.Y.

YOGI BERRA

There may be no sports figure in history that is quoted more than Lawrence Peter "Yogi" Berra. His malapropisms are legendary, and given near Buddha-like status not just among sports fans, but in the advertising and business world as well. Yogi may not have always known what he was saying, but he often managed to put things in a way that required some thought to actually see the merit of his words. Other times, though, it was just sheer nonsense, but always entertaining. And while Berra made his mark as a major league ballplayer, he spent parts of six seasons as a major league manager with both New York teams—the Yankees and the Mets—and is one of the few managers in history to win pennants in both the American and National Leagues.

Lawrence Peter Berra was born in 1925 in St. Louis, Missouri. He grew up like most kids in the neighborhood, playing baseball, and was eventually good enough to be signed by the Yankees. After a stint in the U.S. Navy in World

War II, Berra, an outfielder, joined Newark in the International League in 1946. He was called up with the Yankees the following season, and would later be converted to a full-time catcher. He was behind the plate for the Yankees for much of the time from 1949 to 1959, and then spent his latter years splitting time between catching and the outfield before he retired after the 1963 season. Berra retired with Hall of Fame career numbers: 358 home runs, 1,430 runs batted in, and a .285 average. He was a three-time Most Valuable Player in the American League, and was the anchor of most of the 10 World Series championship teams on which he played for the Yankees. He played in an unmatched 14 World Series and holds series records for games (75), at-bats (259), hits (71), and doubles (10).

Immediately after his retirement, Berra began his second career as a manager with the Yankees. He led the Yankees to the 1964 American League pennant, but lost to the St. Louis Cardinals in seven games in the World Series, and was fired for his efforts after just one year. He was a favorite of former Yankee manager Casey Stengel, though, and Stengel brought him over to the Mets coaching staff. When Mets manager Gil Hodges died from a heart attack in 1972, Berra took over as the Mets manager. He led them to an improbable National League pennant in the 1973 "You Gotta Believe" season, when the Mets came back from what had been a disappointing year to win the NL East, and then to defeat the mighty Cincinnati Reds in five games in the NL Championship Series. They would go on to lose to the Oakland Athletics in seven games in the World Series.

Two years later, Berra was fired as the Mets manager, and went crosstown back to the Yankees as a coach. And he would get another chance at managing his old team when he was hired by George Steinbrenner to manage the Yankees in 1983. But he was fired just one month into the 1985 season, and the firing created some bad blood between Berra and Steinbrenner. Berra refused to ever step foot in Yankee Stadium again as long as Steinbrenner owned the team. However, numerous efforts to make amends by Steinbrenner finally paid off during the Yankees recent championship run, and Berra—now the greatest living Yankee, with the passing of Joe DiMaggio and Mickey Mantle—has come back to the stadium for events and ceremonies. He is a success as a player, manager (484-444 career record), and baseball icon.

YOGI BERRA ON:

APPRECIATION

"I'm a lucky guy and I'm happy to be with the Yankees. And I want to thank everyone for making this night necessary."

BASEBALL

"If people don't want to come out to the ballpark, how are you going to stop them?"

"In baseball, you don't know nothing."

"The game isn't over until it's over."

CROWDS

"Nobody goes there anymore because it's too crowded."

FUTURE

"You've got to be very careful if you don't know where you are going because you might not get there."

EDUCATION

"I'm not going to buy my kids an encyclopedia. Let them walk to school like I did."

"Bill Dickey is learning me his experience."

FOOD

"You better cut the pizza in four pieces because I'm not hungry enough to eat six."

HALL OF FAME

"What's good about the Hall of Fame is you get to see the guys you never see."

HITTING

"He hits from both sides of the plate. He's amphibious."

"How can you hit and think at the same time?"

"I never blame myself when I'm not hitting. I just blame the bat and if it keeps up, I change bats. After all, if I know it isn't my fault that I'm not hitting, how can I get mad at myself?"

HONORS

"When you're a great enough person, you get to be a place."

LITTLE LEAGUE

"I think Little League is wonderful. It keeps the kids out of the house."

"Little League baseball is a very good thing because it keeps the parents off the streets."

LOOKS

"So I'm ugly. I never saw anyone hit with his face."

MANAGING

"I can be tough if I have to. I just don't think yelling at players does any good. I'd rather take a guy over to the side quietly and tell him if he does something wrong."

"In this job, you probably have to get fired sooner or later."

"It ain't like football. You can't make up no trick plays."

MARRIAGE

"We have a good time together, even when we're not together."

MATH

"Baseball is 90 percent mental. The other half is physical."

"You give 100 percent in the first half of the game, and if that isn't enough, in the second half you give what's left."

MISTAKES

"We made too many wrong mistakes."

MONEY

"A nickel ain't worth a dime anymore."

"You know me all this time, and you can't spell my name?"

—After receiving a check from appearing on the post-game radio show, issued to "Pay to Bearer"

"Why buy good luggage? You only use it when you travel."

MUSIC

"Hey, Linz, take that harmonica and stuff it."

—The famous harmonica incident of the 1964 New York Yankees, when Yogi told infielder Phil Linz to stop playing the harmonica on the team bus. Linz tossed the harmonica at Yogi, and he threw it back, hitting Joe Pepitone in the leg.

PEOPLE

"You can observe a lot just by watching."

"You should always go to other people's funerals, otherwise, they won't come to yours."

PERSPECTIVE

"I ate good today, and look, I even got paid."

—After suffering through a losing streak managing the Yankees in 1964

"If the world were perfect it wouldn't be."

"We were overwhelming underdogs."

"When you come to a fork in the road, take it."

PITCHERS

"All pitchers are liars or crybabies."

"I can see how he [Sandy Koufax] won 25 games. What I don't understand is how he lost five."

RECORDS

"I always thought that record would stand until it was broken."

SLEEP

"If I didn't wake up, I'd still be sleeping."

SLUMPS

"Slump? I ain't in no slump. I just ain't hitting."

STREAKING

"I don't know [if they were men or women fans running naked across the field]. They had bags over their heads."

TALKING

"I never said most of the things I said."

"Public speaking is one of the things I hate the best."

"It was impossible to get a conversation going, everybody was talking too much."

"These things just come out. I can't plan 'em. I don't even know I say 'em myself."

TIME

"It gets late early out there."

"It's like deja vu all over again."

"I knew I was going to take the wrong train, so I left early."

UMPIRES

"Anybody who can't hear the difference between a ball hitting wood and a ball hitting concrete must be blind."

WEATHER

"It ain't the heat, it's the humility."

"You don't look so hot yourself."

—Yogi responding to a woman who commented that he looked "mighty cool"

WINNING

"You can't win all the time. There are guys out there who are better than you."

YANKEES

"I'd rather be the Yankee catcher than president."

College Football Hall of Fame
South Bend, Ind.

BOBBY BOWDEN

Bobby Bowden was born as a son of the South, on November 8, 1929, in Birmingham, Alabama Football became a passion for him at a young age, but that passion was nearly snuffed out when, at the age of 13, he contracted rheumatic fever and was bedridden for more than a year. However, he eventually recovered and went on to become a star football player at Woodlawn High School in Birmingham.

He grew up dreaming of playing football at the University of Alabama, and he fulfilled that dream, playing at Alabama as a freshman quarterback. However, after one semester, he missed the love of his life—his childhood sweetheart, Ann Estock—and returned to Birmingham to marry her. Bowden transferred to Howard University (now known as Samford University), where he became a Little All-American quarterback in 1952.

Bowden began his head coaching career right in Birmingham, at his alma mater, and had immediate success, posting a 31-6 record at Samford University from 1959 to 1962. His next head coaching job was at West Virginia University, where Bowden began to solidify his success as a major college coach, with a 42-26 record from 1970 to 1975. But it was his next stop where Bobby Bowden would create one of the most remarkable winning legacies in college football.

Since he was hired at Florida State University, Bowden's teams have won 10 or more games 18 times. Before he arrived, the Seminoles had been to just eight bowl games in 29 years. Under Bowden, FSU has appeared in 23 bowl games and has won two national championships. The Seminoles are the only team ranked in the Associated Press Top Five for 15 consecutive seasons. They have the winningest college football program in the 1990s, and won more games in the decade of the 90s (108) than any team has over any previous decade in NCAA history. Bowden's record at Florida State is 250-59-4, and he has won a total of 323 games over his college football coaching career.

His football legacy has extended to his sons. Tommy Bowden is the head coach at Clemson University, and Terry Bowden is a college football television analyst for ABC and was head coach at Auburn University. Another son, Jeff, is on Bowden's staff at FSU.

Bowden's profile has only been raised by his colorful and often quotable style of talking, and he remains a sought-after speaker throughout the country.

BOBBY BOWDEN ON:

ATTITUDE

"I think people are good before I think they are bad. Too many people, the first time they see somebody, they don't like them right away. My first reaction is I like them."

AWARDS

"I've had Coach of the Year honors. I could care less about them. It doesn't mean a thing to me. My fun is winning a game. Being national champion is like the heavyweight crown. Coach of the Year and that stuff does not turn me on.

If I had to choose between winning the conference and winning an honor, it wouldn't even be close."

BIGOTRY

"Racial bigotry is nothing but pure ignorance, not to mention hate, and if my vocabulary was bigger, I could probably come up with some better words to describe it."

CHARACTER

"The type of players we recruit are the same type we recruited 20 years ago when we won the Sunday school award. We recruit the best kids we can, if they're bad characters, we don't sign them. It's not your bad guys that are bad all the time. It's your good guys who go out and do something wrong just like you and I did when we were kids. The difference is everybody knows about it now."

"Dependability, hard work, and a boy who honors his father and mother."

COACHING

"I just love to coach. That may sound simple, but I think sometimes people like the things that go around coaching and not the actual job. I have always gotten my greatest pleasure out of breaking down film, learning about opponents and yourself, then implementing a game plan to take advantage of your strengths and their weaknesses. I love to take a group of young men in the late summer and mold them into a team."

"I can't wait to go to work every morning. I can't remember a morning when I didn't want to go to work."

DESIRE

"When I go after something, I go after it hard. It has always been that way. I don't know. It's in my blood."

DISCIPLINE

"I usually frighten the kid once. I have 85 scholarship players; therefore, you have to keep the team solid. If I've got a boy who violates a rule, whether against the university, or downtown, or some girl, or a bank or something, I'll usually try to defend him the first time. If it's turned over to me, I'll try to save him somehow. I'll punish him, try to give him a real bad punishment so he won't do it again. If he does it twice, I tell him he's gone."

"You don't want them to feel like they're in prison."

—*Talking about the curfew he set for his team
in New Orleans before the Sugar Bowl*

"Discipline to me is sacrifice. It's a willingness to give up something you want to do, so you can better yourself."

FAITH

"It's better to have faith in a cause that will ultimately succeed than to succeed in a cause that will ultimately fail."

FAMILY

"A lot of people, all they want is a winning football player. We know the boys. We know their mama. We know their daddy. We don't want to lose them. We don't want to see them go bad."

"So many of these kids don't have a daddy. Who's gonna raise these doggone kids if the coaches don't? I don't condone misbehavior. But I don't want to kill my boy. I want him to learn from it."

"We think we do all we can. It's like raising children. No matter how much you teach them and coach them, they've got to make their own decisions."

FOOTBALL

"Football goes in cycles. For 10 years maybe offenses will dominate. They'll be so tough, the defense won't know how to handle it. All of a sudden, the defense will handle that, and for 10 years we'll have a defensive cycle. You have to stay up with it. You look at film to try to find something that will counter it, that will work, beat it. It causes new ideas. Sometimes they are old ideas just brought back up. That happens in most cases. That's why you go to coaching clinics. Every spring, my coaches go to other schools. You try to learn what they are doing. You go to schools that are winning. All kinds of people come to ours."

"Defense might be the most important thing. You have to have a defense good enough not to get you into scoring contests with people because you can't win scoring contests all the time. If you're beating people 35-30 and 42-37, one of them is going to get you before long. If your defense is holding people, you should win. Just like our defense against Oklahoma in the Orange Bowl, they played good enough for us to win. They held them to 13 points. You shouldn't beat us with 13 points. You got to play defense that can keep you from getting in shooting contests."

HEALTH

"If you can stay healthy, that's the name of the game. There's no reason you can't stay successful if you stay healthy."

JOB SECURITY

"Fear creeps in. Are they going to fire me? Are my wife and children hearing all this trash? It made me work hard, I guess. The next year at West Virginia, we had a good year and went to a bowl, won the bowl, and because of it, I was offered the Florida State job. So I learned something that year that has transformed my thinking. I've always been a deep loyalist. When I join something, I'm going to stay with it. When I was head coach at West Virginia for three or four years, I thought I'd probably be there the rest of my career. They gave me a job, I'm going to do my best and stay here. Then we had that losing season, 4-7, and I saw the people turn. 'Goodbye Bobby.' It told me, Bobby, if you get a better job offer, take it if you want it. You have every right in the world to take it, because these people have already shown you they will forsake you."

"Some folks used to say I had a halo over my head but I always knew, with just a little slippage, it could become a noose."

LIFE

"Life isn't fair, because if it were, God would strike me dead where I stand, and no innocent baby would ever die."

LOSING

"If I take a bad licking, I can't wait to get it straightened out. What did I do wrong? How can I change this? How can we turn this ship around? That's the whole motivating thing in coaching."

"I haven't even got a speech for this."

—Reacting to FSU's 41-9 loss to Florida after the Seminoles turned the ball over five times

MILITARY

"My heroes were the MacArthurs, the Pattons, the Bradleys. I can relate it to myself in coaching. I've had a lot of people tell me, 'You would have been like them. They were driven by audacity.' They tried some things people wouldn't think they'd try."

MISTAKES

"The greatest mistake is to continue to practice a mistake."

MONEY

"I don't think I could coach a guy making $2 million. I tell him something, he'll say, 'Hey, go jump in the lake. I got more money than you got.'"

MOTIVATION

"It's kind of interesting as to what motivates people, because everybody is motivated by something. Mine has always been the motivation of fear. I coach as hard as I can in order to keep from losing. When we lose a game, it hurts many times more than a win feels good. When you win a ball game, 24 hours and it's over. When you lose, it dwells with you for years. You wonder, could I have done this or that differently?"

PUBLICITY

"If you don't want people to know about it, don't be number one, be number 50. Then nobody will learn about you. This I have found out."

SPORTSMANSHIP

"Sportsmanship to me is going out and playing as hard as you can within the rules."

Teamwork

"If you get the best players, you're going to get the kids who have egos. You have to take the 'I' concept out and get the 'we' concept."

"Our motto is: 'It's not about me.' In other words, you have to put yourself last in this thing. It's the team first."

Trouble

"If I have a kid who commits murder, I gotta let him go."

"If I told you some of the things I did, they wouldn't even let me come back here in a year. There were a lot of windows busted out that I might have had a little something to do with. A lot of street lights knocked out, things like that."

"Sometimes you have to wait for the school to make a decision because it involves them. Sometimes you have to wait for the local police force to make a decision because it involves them. So sometimes it doesn't even get to you. But let's say it's an issue they wanted you to handle. Then there are two things you've got to consider: your university, which I guess has to come first; but we coaches also consider the individual, which sometimes other people could care less about."

"If I got a kid who goes out and gets a good discount, I want to know how he did it."

—Referring to the shopping spree by Florida State receiver Peter Warrick, in which Warrick paid about $20 for more than $400 worth of merchandise

VALUES

"My family is more important than football, and my religion is more important than either one."

WINNING

"The winning doesn't feel as good as the losing does bad."

"I am not happy with moral victories. Those are forgotten."

College Football Hall of Fame
South Bend, Ind.

BEAR BRYANT

Paul Williams Bryant was born on September 11, 1913, in Moro Bottom, Arkansas, the 11th of 12 children. "Bear" Bryant was born later at a local theater when Paul Williams Bryant took up the challenge to wrestle a bear. And the Bear's football education began on the high school fields of Arkansas, where he was an all-state player.

Bryant would go on to play college football at the place where his destiny for greatness laid ahead of him—at the University of Alabama, where the teams he played on won two Southeastern Conference titles in 1933 and 1934. He began his great coaching legacy after he graduated in 1935, as a head coach at tiny Union College in Jackson, Tennessee. Shortly after, he went back to Alabama as an assistant coach for three years.

Moving on to Vanderbilt for two seasons as an assistant, Bryant joined the U.S. Navy in 1941 to serve his country. When he got out of the service in 1945, Bryant came north to Maryland for his first job running a program in

1945. He was a strict disciplinarian right from the start, and in demand early. After posting a 6-2-1 record at Maryland, Bryant moved on to Kentucky the following season, where he spent seven years building his reputation as one of brightest young coaches in the college ranks. Bryant coached the Wildcats to four bowl games and their first Southeastern Conference title.

In 1954, Bryant moved on to coach at Texas A&M, and two years later led them to the Southwest Conference championship. He had been a winner wherever he went, and it was time to go home. The Crimson Tide football program had fallen on hard times, and called on the 44-year-old Bryant to return to his alma mater to build it back up. He wound up taking it to the greatest heights a program has ever seen.

Within three years, Bryant brought a national championship to Alabama, the first one coming in 1961, followed by five more national titles in 1964, 1965, 1973, 1978, and 1979. He coached great ballplayers along the way such as Joe Namath and Ken Stabler, and became a national icon for both his winning ways and his quotable style of speaking—almost a national wise man.

He was able to capture the attention of the national media with his Southern drawl, the words that he used with that homespun delivery, and also the love and devotion of his players. The story goes that one Alabama professor, after seeing the players react to a pregame pep talk by Bryant, said, "If I could reach my students like that, I'd teach for nothing."

In 1981, Bryant reached an unparalleled level of immortality when he broke Amos Alonzo Stagg's record of 314 career victories, and would finish with 323 career wins (323-85-17) when he retired in 1982, after 25 winning seasons and 24 bowl appearances. Bryant died shortly after retiring on January 26, 1983.

BEAR BRYANT ON:

ACADEMICS

"How many people watch you give a final exam? Well, I have 50,000 watch me give mine—every Saturday!"

—Giving a Texas A&M English Professor a reality check after the professor, who said he had about 50 in a class, complained about Bryant's demands on winning and the salary the football coach earned

ADVERSITY

"You never know how a horse will pull until you hook him up to a heavy load."

"In life, you'll have your back up against the wall many times. You might as well get used to it."

ALABAMA

"I just want to thank God for giving me the opportunity to coach at my alma mater and be part of the University of Alabama tradition."

"I left Texas A&M because my school called me. Mama called, and when Mama calls, then you just have to come running."

—On why he left Texas A&M with six years remaining on his contract to coach at Alabama

"What are you doing here? Tell me why you are here. If you are not here to win a national championship, you're in the wrong place. You boys are special. I don't want my players to be like other students. I want special people. You can learn a lot on the football field that isn't taught in the home, the church, or the classroom. There are going to be days when you think you've got no more to give and then you're going to give plenty more. You are going to have pride and class. You are going to be very special. You are going to win the national championship for Alabama."

—*Speaking to his first football team at Alabama*

ATTITUDE

"Smile. You'll catch a lot more bugs if you smile than you will with vinegar."

"I think the most important thing of all for any team is a winning attitude. The coaches must have it. The players must have it. The student body must have it. If you have dedicated players who believe in themselves, you don't need a lot of talent."

"Put everything you've got into anything you do."

"Set a goal, adopt a plan that will help you to achieve the goal. Chances of things happening in this world without goals are slim. Make sure that the goal means a lot to you. Believe that the plan is going to win. Tie to people who believe in the plan."

AUBURN

"I know one thing, I'd rather die now than to have died this morning and missed this game."

—*After Alabama's after win over unbeaten Auburn in '71*

"What the hell's the matter with you people down there? Don't y'all take your football seriously?"

> *—After calling Auburn at 6 a.m. one day only to find out that none of the coaches were at work yet*

BOWLS

"Woody is a great coach...and I ain't bad."

> *—Commenting on rival coach Woody Hayes after Alabama defeated Ohio State 35-8 in the 1978 Sugar Bowl*

CHARACTER

"I have tried to teach them to show class, to have pride, and to display character. I think football and winning games takes care of itself if you do that."

"There's no substitute for guts."

COACHING

"Mama wanted me to be a preacher. I told her coaching and preaching were a lot alike."

"I don't pay attention to a coach. I've never seen a coach win a game yet."

"Don't do a lot of coaching just before the game. If you haven't coached them by 14 minutes to 2 on Saturday, it's too late then."

DESIRE

"You're still going to win with preparation and dedication and plain old desire. If you don't have genuine desire, you won't be dedicated enough to prepare properly."

DETERMINATION

"What matters...is not the size of the dog in the fight, but of the fight in the dog."

"If you believe in yourself and have dedication and pride—and never quit, you'll be a winner. The price of victory is high, but so are the rewards."

FOOTBALL

"Only three things can happen on a pass play, and two of them are bad."

"Offense sells tickets. Defense wins games."

"Some coaches have accused me of being too defense-minded, but most of those who said that have wound up being athletic directors."

LOSING

"When you win, there's glory enough for everybody. When you lose, there's glory for none."

"Losing doesn't make me want to quit. It makes me want to fight that much harder."

MOTIVATION

"Regardless of who was coaching them, they still would have been a great team. I said early in the season that they were the nicest, even sissiest, bunch I ever had. I think they read it, because later on they got unfriendly."

—Talking about his 1961 national championship team

"I'm just a simple plowhand from Arkansas, but I have learned over the years how to hold a team together. How to lift some men up, how to calm others down, until finally they've got one heartbeat, together, a team."

"Every man I had left on the team felt he could whip Joe Louis on Saturday."

"Football has never been just a game to me. Never. I knew it from the time it got me out of Moro Bottom, Arkansas— and that's one of the things that motivated me, that fear of going back to plowing and driving those mules and chopping cotton for 50 cents a day."

PLAYERS

"Players can be divided up, roughly, into four types. Those who have ability and know it, those who have it and don't know it, those who don't have it and know it, and those who don't have it but don't know it."

"The one that makes you proud is the one who isn't good enough to play, but it means so much to him, he puts so much into it, that he plays anyway. I have had a lot of those, and I can coach them better than most."

"Stephenson was a man among children; he didn't say very much, but he didn't have to."

—*Talking about Dwight Stephenson, the center on his 1979 Alabama national championship team*

"Lee Roy was the best college linebacker—bar none. He would have made every tackle on every play if they had stayed in bounds."

—*Talking about Alabama linebacker Lee Roy Jordan*

"He can't run, he can't pass, and he can't kick—all he can do is beat you."

—*Speaking about Alabama quarterback Pat Trammel*

"This is the saddest day of my life."

—*After learning that Pat Trammell had died of cancer in December 1968*

"I didn't care if we ever quit practicing. I loved it. The only other guy I ever knew who loved it as much was Jerry Duncan. He would beg to practice even when he was hurt. I've actually seen him cry because the trainer told him he couldn't scrimmage."

—*Speaking about Alabama tackle Jerry Duncan*

SPORTSWRITERS

"Here's a 20, bury two."

—*When asked to contribute $10 to help pay for the costs of a sportswriter's funeral*

THE LEGEND

"Well, I won't say if I can or I can't. But if I do, I do it before most people get up in the morning."

—When asked if it was true he could walk on water

THE RECORD

"All I know is, I don't want to stop coaching, and I don't want to stop winning, so we're gonna break the record unless I die."

—When asked if he would break Amos Alonzo Stagg's record of 314 college wins

TIES

"Hell, no! A tie is like kissing your sister!"

—After being asked if he had considered going for a field goal when trailing by three points

WINNING

"I ain't never been nothin' but a winner."

"I don't know if I'm smart enough to know how to describe a winner, but I guess I've been wise enough or maybe just lucky enough to be able to spot one. I know a winner has dedication and pride and the will to win, and he'll do a little bit extra every day to improve himself and his team. A winner is worried about his team and his school, and he'll outwork people, and he'll sacrifice."

"If wanting to win is a fault, as some of my critics seem to insist, then I plead guilty. I like to win. I know no other way. It's in my blood."

WHAT OTHERS HAVE SAID ABOUT BEAR BRYANT:

"You go by that and they'll have to fire us all."

> —*Auburn head coach Shug Jordan after learning that LSU coach Charlie McLendon was fired for not being able to beat Alabama*

"I can't imagine being in the Hall of Fame with Coach Bryant. There ought to be two Hall of Fames, one for Coach Bryant and one for everybody else."

> —*Former Alabama receiver Ozzie Newsome when he was inducted into the Alabama Hall of Fame*

"I'd do it again in a minute. If you're a football player, you dream of playing for Coach Bryant."

> —*John Mitchell, the first black player to play football at Alabama*

"He literally knocked the door down. I mean right off its hinges. A policeman came in and asked who knocked the door down, and Coach Bryant said, 'I did.' The policeman just said, 'Okay,' and walked off."

> —*Alabama tackle Jerry Duncan recalling an irate Bryant after a 7-7 tie with Tennessee*

"This must be what God looks like."

> —*Quarterback George Blanda, who played for Bryant at Kentucky, talking about the first time he ever met the coach*

"He literally coached himself to death. He was our greatest coach."

> —*Former Ohio State head coach Woody Hayes, speaking at the funeral for Bear Bryant*

CARDS

"Coaches are an integral part of any manager's team, especially if they are good pinochle players."

—Baseball manager Earl Weaver

CHALLENGES

"How you respond to the challenge in the second half will determine what you become after the game, whether you are a winner or a loser."

—Basketball coach Pat Riley

CHAMPIONS

"The vision of a champion is someone who is bent over, drenched in sweat, at the point of exhaustion when no one else is watching."

—Soccer coach Anson Dorrance

CHAMPIONSHIPS

"The team that gets off to a good start wins pennants."

> —*Baseball manager John McGraw on the benefits of an early start in a championship season*

"There was no doubt in Tom Osborne's mind, and there was no doubt in my mind. It was a championship game, and he went after it like a champion."

> —*University of Miami football coach Howard Schnellenberger on Tom Osborne's decision to go for two instead of kicking the tying point that would have given Nebraska the national championship*

"The only thing bad about winning the pennant is that you have to manage the All-Star Game the next year. I'd rather go fishing for three years."

> —*Baseball manager Whitey Herzog on one of the drawbacks of winning a championship.*

"When your are playing for the national championship, it's not a matter of life or death. It's more important than that."

> —*Football coach Duffy Daugherty*

"We had more impact than you would ever think on our young, on our old, and the way people feel about themselves, each other, and their city."

> —*Football coach Bill Walsh on the impact his championship 49ers had on San Francisco*

"If I'd known it was going to take 25 years [to get to the Stanley Cup final], I'd have started earlier."

> —*Dallas Stars hockey coach Ken Hitchcock*

Character

"It is not the honor that you take with you, but the heritage you leave behind."

—Baseball manager and general manager Branch Rickey

Cheating

"He [Don Drysdale] talks very well for a guy who's had two fingers in his mouth all his life."

—Baseball manager Gene Mauch

"I've cheated, or someone on my team has cheated, in almost every single game I've been in."

—Baseball manager Roger Hornsby,
bragging about cheating

"If you can cheat, I wouldn't wait one pitch longer."

—Baseball manager George Bamberger, speaking
to pitcher Ross Grimsley on the mound

"He [Gaylord Perry] should be in the Hall of Fame with a tube of KY jelly attached to his plaque."

—Baseball manager Gene Mauch

"They'll fire you for losing before they'll fire you for cheating."

—Football coach Darryl Rogers

"If you know how to cheat, start now."

—Baseball manager Earl Weaver

CLOTHES

"I'm fat and I sweat a lot and don't want to ruin all my clothes."

> *—Basketball coach Don Haskins when asked*
> *why he wears the same clothes*

"With all those guys in suits and ties on the bench, the sideline was beginning to look like the men's shop at Macy's."

> *—LSU basketball coach Dale Brown on why*
> *he reduced his assistant coaching staff*

"That's part of wearing pants or wearing a skirt. That is why people have a problem with this DH stuff. A lot of times a pitcher can wear a skirt. I'm not trying to be chauvinistic, but I guess I was."

> *—New York Mets manager Bobby Valentine, on pitcher*
> *Roger Clemens throwing at Mets catcher Mike Piazza*

COACHING

"Work hard, stay focused, and surround yourself with good people."

> *—Nebraska football coach Tom Osborne*

"You must have a passion to coach."

> *—Basketball coach Rick Majerus*

"A coach is often responsible to an irresponsible public."

> *—Football coach Bob Zuppke*

"Other people go to the office. I get to coach. I know I've been blessed."

> *—North Carolina State basketball coach Jim Valvano*

"I want my teams to have my personality: surly, obnoxious, and arrogant."

—*Basketball coach Al McGuire*

"Coaching is like being a king. It prepares you for nothing."

—*Hockey coach Herb Brooks*

"People think there are great mysteries connected with the game, but there are not. It's just teaching fundamentals."

—*NFL coach and owner Paul Brown*

"This is a 1,000-mile journey, and every 10 minutes people want to know if we're there yet. No, we're not where we want to be. Evolution has to take place."

—*Basketball coach Jim Cleamons*

"Coaches are like ducks. Calm on top, but paddling underneath. Believe me, there's a lot of leg movement."

—*Hockey coach Ken Hitchcock*

"All coaches are in their last year of their contract, only some of them don't know it yet."

—*Football coach Dan Henning*

"Behind every fired football coach stands a college president."

—*Football coach John McKay*

"A lot of guys go through their whole careers and don't win a championship, but are still great coaches."

—*Basketball coach Chuck Daly*

"Maybe one of the qualities of being a great coach is being [a jerk]. There are quite a few of them around."

—*Hockey coach Larry Robinson*

"I think what coaching is all about is taking players and analyzing their ability and put them in a position where they can excel within the framework of the team winning."

—*Football coach Don Shula*

"The trouble with most coaches is they want to make the game too damn complicated."

—*Football coach Buddy Parker*

"Coaching is easy. Winning is the hard part."

—*Basketball coach and player Elgin Baylor*

"When I was coaching, the one thought that I would try to get across to my players was that everything I do each day, everything I say, I must first think what effect it will have on everyone concerned."

—*Basketball coach Frank Layden*

"Leisure time is that five or six hours when you sleep at night."

—*NFL coach George Allen on the time coaching demands*

"Don't worry about the horse being blind. Just load up the wagon.

—*Football coach and sportscaster John Madden talking about the message he gave his players before every game. He later admitted he had no clue what the message meant*

"Play against the Game, not your opponent."

—*Oklahoma football coach Bud Wilkinson*

"A coach can't be concerned with the poor ballplayer. If the player can't make it, he's got to be out right away. It's a very tough aspect of coaching, and in this aspect I was weak. Also, some guys get fat on coaching, they get healthy and strong, but other guys get ulcers."

—Football coach Johnny Blood

"There are only two kinds of coaches: those who have been fired and those who will be fired."

—Basketball coach Ken Loeffler

"Systems win! Believe in your system, and then sell it to your players."

—Basketball coach Billy Donovan

"If an assistant doesn't buy your philosophy, one of you won't be there long."

—Basketball coach Roy Thompson

"The coach who thinks his coaching is more important than his talent is an idiot."

—Basketball coach Joe Lapchick

"When I walked out, I couldn't feel my legs. I tried to act cool, but I was afraid I might trip over a line. I was just glad to get to the bench and sit down."

—Indiana basketball coach Mike Davis on his first game after replacing Bobby Knight

"All really successful coaches have a system."

—North Carolina State basketball coach Jim Valvano

"A football coach's most important job is evaluation of players."

—*Football coach and television analyst Lee Corso*

"You need to be as distinctive as you can. Rather than say, 'Throw it to him,' we would say, 'Throw it to the numbers,' or 'Throw it to the outside of where the defender was.' You want to try to be as specific as you can, so then you have a reference point."

—*Football coach Bill Walsh*

"You have to convince your players that the only reason a play failed was that they didn't execute properly."

—*Football coach Bill McCartney*

"The key to your success will be not what you do, but how well you teach what you do."

—*Football coach John Robinson*

"Once you have a plan, you must sell it to the players. It is not enough to put it on the blackboard and say, 'Okay, here it is.' You have to convince the players that the plan is a good one and show them, in specific ways, why it will work. If you do, you send them out to the practice field with more confidence."

—*Football coach Joe Gibbs*

"We watch the good things you do so you can see why and how you did them. We watch the average things so you can improve on them, and we watch the bad things you do so you won't do them again."

—*Football coach and television analyst John Madden*

"If a coach is determined to stay in the coaching profession, he will develop from year to year. This much is true, no coach has a monopoly on the knowledge of basketball. There are no secrets in the game. The only secrets, if there are any, are good teaching of sound fundamentals, intelligent handling of men, a sound system of play, and the ability to instill in the boys a desire to win."

—*Kentucky basketball coach Adolph Rupp*

"As coaches, we represent one of the few remaining organized systems for demanding discipline of young men. Their education will not be complete if it does not include the discipline and generosity that can come from being a team member, if it does not include an awareness of responsibility to others. We are 'people coaches,' not just 'football coaches.'"

—*Football coach Ara Parseghian*

"There are a lot of good football coaches. But I want great people around me. I want to enjoy coaching. I don't want to have to fight and argue all the time."

—*Football coach Bob Toledo*

"A good coach will make his players see what they can be rather than what they are."

—*Football coach Ara Parseghian*

COMMISSIONERS

"What did the search committee decide? Not to search?"

—*New York Mets manager Bobby Valentine, upon learning that Bud Selig would become baseball's full-time commissioner*

COMMITTEES

"A committee is usually a group of uninformed, appointed by the unwilling, to accomplish the unnecessary."

—Baseball general manager Syd Thrift

COMMITMENT

"There are only two options regarding commitment. You're either in or you're out. There's no such thing as life in-between."

—Basketball coach Pat Riley

"Commitment is like ham and eggs. The chicken makes a contribution. The pig makes a commitment."

—Hockey coach Fred Shero

"If you don't make a total commitment to whatever you're doing, then you start looking to bail out the first time the boat starts leaking. It's tough enough getting that boat to shore with everybody rowing, let alone when a guy stands up and starts putting his jacket on."

—Football coach Lou Holtz

COMMUNICATION

"Your ability to communicate to your young people will determine your success."

—Basketball coach Jim Harrick

COMPETITION

"As long as I've got a chance to beat you, I'm going to take it."

—Baseball manager Leo Durocher on his intense competitive nature

"Buy a steak for a player on another club after the game, but don't even speak to him on the field. Get out there and beat them to death."

—Baseball manager Leo Durocher on players fraternizing on the field

"Give me some scratching, diving, hungry ballplayers who come to kill you."

—Baseball manager Leo Durocher on what he wants in his ballplayers

"If I were playing third base and my mother were rounding third with the run that was going to beat us, I'd trip her. Oh, I'd pick her up and brush her off and say, 'Sorry, Mom,' but nobody beats me."

—Baseball manager Leo Durocher, expressing his love for his mother

"It is better to be devoured by lions than to be eaten by dogs."

—Northwestern football coach Alex Agase, on why his team played tough schedules

"I don't care how good you play, you can find somebody who can beat you, and I don't care how bad you play, you can find somebody you can beat."

—Golf coach Harvey Penick

"How you respond to the challenge in the second half will determine what you become after the game, whether you are a winner or a loser."

—*Football coach Lou Holtz*

"Competitive. People say that about me, that makes me feel good."

—*Football coach Steve Spurrier*

COMPLAINING

"I can't stand it when a player whines to me or his teammates or his wife or the writers or anyone else. A whiner is almost always wrong. A winner never whines."

—*NFL coach and owner Paul Brown,*
on his distaste for complainers

CONFIDENCE

"Before you can win, you have to believe you are worthy."

—*Football coach Mike Ditka*

CONSISTENCY

"It's how well the *average* player performs that gives your team consistency and substance."

—*Football coach Eddie Crowder*

CREDIT

"I'll borrow from anybody, but once I use it, it's mine."

—Football coach Wayne Hardin

CRIME

"That's great. We'll take 29 players, and let the muggers make our final cuts."

—New York Mets manager Bobby Valentine, after learning his team would play two exhibition games in New Orleans before the regular season began

CRITICISM

"The only players I hurt with my words are the ones who have an inflated opinion of their ability."

—Football coach Bill Parcells

CURSING

"I'll never forget one of his pep talks before a Lakers game. There were 72 bleeps in it and it was Christmas Day."

—Boston Celtic player Paul Westphal, describing one of the pep talks by Celtics coach Tommy Heinsohn

"I cussed him out in Spanish and he threw me out in English."

—Baseball manager Lou Piniella after being tossed out of a game by an umpire

DANCING

"I don't think you can really trust a man who likes to dance."

—*Football coach Brian Billick*

DEATH

"I don't want to achieve immortality by making the Hall of Fame. I want to achieve immortality by not dying."

—*Baseball manager Leo Durocher*

"They can put on my tombstone, 'He'd a lasted a lot longer if he hadn't played Pittsburgh six times in two years.'"

—*Football coach Bum Phillips*

"You can have money stacked to the ceiling, but the size of your funeral is still going to depend upon the weather."

—*Baseball manager Chuck Tanner*

DEDICATION

"The bigger the price you pay for something, the harder it is to give up on it."

—Basketball coach Bob Williams

DEFEAT

"I think everyone should experience defeat at least once during their career. You learn a lot from it."

—Football coach Lou Holtz

"If the day ever comes when I can swallow defeat, I'll quit."

—Hockey coach Toe Blake

DEFENSE

"What counts aren't the number of double plays, but the ones you should have had and missed."

—Baseball manager Whitey Herzog
on the value of good defense

DEMONS

"I said it was time someone stole the broomstick of the Wicked Witch. I'm really happy for our guys. They were carrying all those demons around."

—Washington Capitals hockey coach Ron Wilson referred
to one of his favorite movies, The Wizard of Oz *in a*
motivational speech to his players, exhorting them
to atone for past playoff failures

DESIRE

"The worst thing is the day you realize you want to win more than the players do."

—*Baseball manager Gene Mauch*

"Never underestimate the heart of a champion."

—*Basketball coach Rudy Tomjanovich*

"I believe in playing with your heart, with every fiber in your body—fairly, squarely, by the rules—to win. And I believe that any man's finest moment, the greatest fulfillment of all he holds dear, is that moment when he has worked his heart out and lies exhausted on the floor of battle—victorious."

—*Gymnastics coach Bela Karolyi*

"Some of the greatest players on our football team [the Washington Redskins] were free agents. They were the guys that gave their guts and covered those kickoffs and made all the rest of us look good."

—*Football coach Joe Gibbs*

DETAILS

"In the successful organization, no detail is too small to escape close attention."

—*Football coach Lou Holtz*

DETERMINATION

"What the mind can conceive, the mind can achieve, and those who stay will be champions."

—Michigan football coach Bo Schembechler

"Always remember, anything is yours if you are willing to pay the price."

—NFL coach George Allen

"Each warrior wants to leave the mark of his will, his signature, on important acts he touches. This is not the voice of ego but of the human spirit, rising up and declaring that it has something to contribute to the solution of the hardest problems, no matter how vexing."

—Basketball coach Pat Riley

"The difference between mediocrity and greatness is extra effort."

—Football coach George Allen

"Nobody who ever gave his best regretted it."

—Chicago Bears owner and coach George Halas

"If you get tough mentally, you can get tough physically and overcome fatigue."

—Basketball coach Pat Riley

"One hundred percent is not enough."

—Football coach George Allen

DISCIPLINE

"I feel more strongly about this than anything else in coaching: Anybody who lacks discipline, who doesn't want to be part of the team, who doesn't want to meet the requirements—has to go. It's that simple."

—Oklahoma football coach Bud Wilkinson

"Discipline is 90 percent anticipation."

—Ohio State football coach Woody Hayes

DREAMS

"It's okay to be dreamers, because we all have dreams."

—Hockey coach Herb Brooks

"You know, Willie Wonka said it best: 'We are the makers of dreams, the dreamers of dreams.' We grew up as kids having dreams, but now we're too sophisticated as adults, as a nation. We stopped dreaming. We should always have dreams."

—Hockey coach Herb Brooks

DRINKING

"I'd rather him [Grover Alexander] pitch a crucial game for me drunk, then anyone I've ever known sober. He was that good."

—Baseball manager Roger Hornsby on the talent and drinking habits of pitcher Grover Alexander

"God watches over drunks and third basemen."

—Baseball manager Leo Durocher
comparing drunks to third basemen

"Down there [New Athens, Illinois], we've got more taverns than grocery stores. I walked in, threw down a bill and said, 'Give everybody a drink.' Nice gesture I thought, but down the bar somebody yelled, 'Hey big shot, your brother is still a better ballplayer than you are.'"

—Baseball manager Whitey Herzog
on drinking in his hometown

"If any of my players don't take a drink now and then, they'll be gone. You don't play this game on ginger snaps."

—Baseball manager Lou Durocher

"I was a little worried about the drinking, but they assured me they would be drinking everywhere we went."

—Philadelphia hockey coach Roger Neilson after his
team voted to spend four days off in New Orleans

DYNASTIES

"Perhaps the truest axiom in baseball is that the toughest thing to do is repeat."

—Los Angeles Dodgers manager Walt Alston

EDUCATION

"The real shame was that over half of them hadn't even been colored yet."

—Florida football coach Steve Spurrier after hearing that a fire in the Auburn athletic dormitory burned over 30 books

"Monday through Friday they want you to be like Harvard. On Saturday they want you to play like Oklahoma."

—Basketball coach Jim Valvano

"I don't know why people question the academic training of an athlete. Fifty percent of the doctors in this country graduated in the bottom half of their classes."

—Basketball coach Al McGuire

EFFORT

"You get no medals for trying."

—Football coach Bill Parcells

"We don't want to make a loafer into an All-American. We want to screen out the loafers in the first place."

—*University of Washington football coach Don James*

"You're never a loser until you quit trying."

—*Football coach Mike Ditka*

EMOTION

"There was a lot of emotion at the Alamo, and nobody survived."

—*Football coach Ron Meyer*

EXCELLENCE

"Excellence is the gradual result of always striving to do better."

—*Basketball coach Pat Riley*

"Excellence is the unlimited ability to improve the quality of what you have to offer."

—*Basketball coach Rick Pitino*

EXCUSES

"The trouble with athletes today is that they are great at rationalizing. Too many won't stand up and take the blame and admit they didn't produce. When one does, you have a rare man."

—*Basketball coach and television analyst Hubie Brown*

EXPERTS

"An expert is an ordinary fella away from home."

—*Football coach Bum Phillips*

FAITH

"A fellow has to have faith in God above and Rollie Fingers in the bullpen."

—Oakland Athletics manager Alvin Dark referring to his two most important icons

"Have a spiritual basis which guides you in life. Have a philosophy of life to live by."

—Nebraska football coach Tom Osborne

"I called up Dial-A-Prayer, and they hung up on me."

—Football coach Mack Brown

"You do a lot of praying, but most of the time the answer is no."

—Football coach John McKay

"As we look down through history, we find out that God, at certain points, picks very average men and women, and what he does is gives them a life, gives them some talent, surrounds them with great people and guides them to some achievement."

—Football coach Joe Gibbs

93

"It seems God's getting us back for every little thing."

—*Calgary hockey coach Bruce Sutter on his team's woes*

FANS

"Coaches who start listening to fans wind up sitting next to them."

—*Basketball coach Johnny Kerr*

"We formed a booster club in Utah, but by the end of the season it had turned into a terrorist group."

—*Basketball coach Frank Layden*

"It was Brooklyn against the world. They were not only complete fanatics, but they knew baseball like the fans of no other city. It was exciting to play there. It was a treat. I walked into that crummy, flyblown park as Brooklyn manager for nine years, and every time I entered, my pulse quickened and my spirits soared."

—*Baseball manager Leo Durocher
on Brooklyn Dodgers fans*

"Every obnoxious fan has a wife at home who dominates him."

—*Basketball coach Al McGuire*

"When I heard the boos, the first thing I did was look in the stands to make sure my wife and daughter were clapping."

—*Hockey coach Scotty Bowman*

"Fans tend to get too excited by streaks of either kind and I think the press does, too. There should be a happy medium."

—*Los Angeles Dodgers manager Walt Alston*

"I've been in hockey too long not to know we won't be questioned....When you lose two games at home by one goal and some guy comes running out of the stands and lets you know you're part of the anatomy that's not a hand or a foot."

—*New York Rangers hockey coach Colin Campbell*

"Why certainly I'd like to have that fellow who hits a home run every time at bat, who strikes out every opposing batter when he's pitching, who throws strikes to any base or the plate when he's playing outfield, and who's always thinking about two innings ahead just what he'll do to baffle the other team. Any manager would want a guy like that playing for him. The only trouble is to get him to put down his cup of beer and come down out of the stands and do those things."

—*Baseball manager Danny Murtaugh*

"We got all these so-called f------ fans that come out there, Cub fans, that are supposed to be behind you, ripping every f------ thing you do. I'll tell you one f------ thing, I hope we get hotter than f------ s--- just so we can stuff it up them 3,000 f------ people that show up every f------ day. Because, if they're the real Chicago f------ fans they can kiss my f------ a-- right downtown, and print it! They're really really behind you around here. My f------ a--. Nobody's fault here because you guys are writing good. What the f--- am I supposed to do, go out there and let my f------ players get destroyed every day, and be quiet about it? For the f------ nickle and dime people to show up? The m------------ don't even work! That's why they're out at the f------ game. They ought to go out and get a f------ job and find out what it's like to go out and earn a f------ living. Eighty-five percent of the f------ world's working, and the other 15 come out here. A f------ playground for the c----------. Rip them m------------! Rip them f------ c---------- like the f------ players! Those guys busting their f------ a-- and the f------ people boo! And that's the Cubs?! My f------ a--!"

—*Chicago Cubs manager Lee Elia, talking about Cubs fans at Wrigley Field*

"Don't worry, the fans don't start booing until July."

—Baseball manager Earl Weaver

"Instead of getting support, people are still a lot more comfortable with us being an alcoholic because we're kind of funny."

—Washington Capitals hockey coach Ron Wilson
referring to the reaction of Caps fans
to the team's 1998 playoff success

FEAR

"Everyone has some fear. A man who has no fear belongs in a mental hospital, or on special teams."

—Football coach Walt Michaels

FIGHTING

"I'm getting smarter, I finally punched something that couldn't sue me."

—Baseball manager Billy Martin after he broke his finger
from punching a piece of furniture

"I don't throw the first punch. I throw the second four."

—Baseball manager Billy Martin

"The fans love fighting. The players don't mind. The coaches like the fights. What's the big deal?"

—Hockey coach Don Cherry

FLEXIBILITY

"I found out that if you are going to win games, you had better be ready to adapt."

—Hockey coach Scotty Bowman

FOOD

"If the waitress has dirty ankles, the chili should be good."

—Basketball coach Al McGuire

FOOTBALL

"I am alarmed at the subtle invasion of professional football, which is gaining preeminence over baseball. It's unthinkable."

—Baseball manager and general manager Branch Rickey

"Football isn't necessarily won by the best players. It's won by the team with the best attitude."

—Football coach George Allen

"One of the things I love about football is that you have the full run of emotions and pressures. In fact, every chance I get to talk to any young man, I encourage him to get into athletics, football in particular. It shows you yourself. You must function under pressure. A person either faces up to what it takes or he runs away."

—Pittsburgh Steelers coach Chuck Noll

"You don't get hurt running straight ahead, three-yards-and-a-cloud-of-dust offense. I will pound you and pound you until you quit."

—Ohio State coach Woody Hayes

"Played wholeheartedly, football is a soul-satisfying outlet for the rugged, courageous type of boy who likes physical contact. Played halfheartedly, football is a waste of time and energy. Football is no halfway game. To play it, you have to get wet all over."

—Football coach Dana X. Bible

"Football is one-third offense, one-third defense, and one-third special teams."

—Football coach George Allen

"Football is one of our great American games. It is the duty and responsibility of each of us to see that it is kept in its proper perspective, and that it is protected. We should see that it is used to attain the objectives that mean so much to our way of life."

—Georgia Tech football coach Bobby Dodd

"I love football. I think it is the most wonderful game in the world and I despise to lose."

—Football coach Woody Hayes

"If God wanted football to be played in the spring, he wouldn't have invented baseball."

*—Football coach Sam Rutigliano on
the United States Football League*

Friendships

"Friendships are forgotten when the game begins."

—*Baseball manager Alvin Dark*

"My only friend was my dog, and I told my wife a man should have at least two friends. So she bought me another dog."

—*Football coach Pepper Rodgers*

"I'm not buddy-buddy with the players. If they need a buddy, let them buy a dog."

—*Baseball manager Whitey Herzog*

"This Thanksgiving I called all of my friends in the league. It took about 12 seconds."

—*Football coach Jerry Glanville*

Fundamentals

"Build your empire on the firm foundation of the fundamentals."

—*Football coach Lou Holtz*

Pat Orr

EDDIE FUTCH

I n a sport where people often move around by slithering on their stomachs, Eddie Futch walked tall. He was probably the greatest trainer in the history of boxing, having worked with 20 world champions, including some of the greatest of all time including: heavyweight champion Joe Frazier, light heavyweight champion Michael Spink, and lightweight champion Alexis Arguello.

In boxing, a trainer is the coach, the person in charge of the preparation and motivation of the fighter, and nobody was better than Futch. Eddie Futch got his start in the gyms of Detroit after his family moved from Hillsboro, Mississippi, shortly after Futch was born in 1911. He sparred with the likes of a young Joe Louis. Futch had hopes of being a fighter himself, but after an impressive amateur career, he was forced to stop boxing in 1936 after doctors detected a heart murmur. But by then he was already working with other fighters and he was sought for his boxing expertise, so he took the next natural step, which was to train fighters while he worked for the city of Detroit in youth sports.

Futch later moved to the West Coast in the 1950s and began working with fighters there, and fought against the corrupt boxing bosses who ran the trainer's guild until he broke their power, and triumphed when he developed his first World Champion, welterweight Don Jordan, in 1958.

From there, Futch began building his championship resume. He helped Joe Frazier develop a strategy to defeat Muhammad Ali in The Fight of the Century, Ali-Frazier I, in 1971, and saved Frazier when he mercifully stopped the fight in the 14th round of the Thrilla in Manila, Ali-Frazier III, in 1975, when Frazier could no longer see Ali's punches coming. He continued to be Ali's nemesis, training Ken Norton to an upset win over Ali in their first fight, and he trained another great heavyweight champion, Larry Holmes, during his reign.

Perhaps Futch's greatest achievement was his work with Riddick Bowe, whose antics and loss to Lennox Lewis in the 1988 Olympics in Seoul, Korea, had plummeted his stock as a professional. No one wanted to work with Bowe, but Futch saw the potential in the 6-foot 5-inch, 235-pound Bowe, and took him from an amateur to the undisputed heavyweight championship of the world with a tremendous win over Evander Holyfield in November 1992.

Eddie Futch was a trainer of champions, and a man so wise he should have been designated as the country's national wise man. He died in 2001 at the age of 90, but left behind a legacy of training—coaching—that is worth remembering.

EDDIE FUTCH ON:

ADVICE

"Some people like to drive and harangue, but I just like to lead fighters to do what is necessary. Sometimes I can tell them something that will spur them on, but I don't depend on the muzzle philosophy of instruction. It's the content of the advice."

"How important a corner is in a fight depends on who is in the corner. I've heard people in corners say absolutely the wrong thing and could have cost the fighter a fight. If you say the wrong thing, you could cause a loss."

AUTHORITY

"When the fighter tells the trainer where to train, it's time to go. If I'm not in charge, I don't want to be there."

—Deciding to drop Riddick Bowe after the former champion took a beating in his first disqualification win over Andrew Golota

CHAMPIONS

"The hard work starts when you become a champion. Everyone wants a shot at you, and every fight will be tougher than it would have been if you were just another contender."

CHARACTER

"I just could not entertain the thought of being a party to the defeat of either man."

—Explaining why he chose not to pick between two of his fighters, Larry Holmes and Michael Spinks, when they fought each other, turning down a lucrative payday in the process

COMPASSION

"Joe Frazier was a good father and is a good father. He's got a very lovely family. Nice people. I saw how much time, how much of himself he put into his family. He and his kids were very close. They were like brothers and sisters, rather than father and children. I said I just can't see myself letting this man possibly wind up as a vegetable or be injured fatally, not when he had so much to live for, so much to enjoy. That's what was going through my mind in the 14th round."

—Explaining his decision to stop the third Ali-Frazier fight, known as the Thrilla in Manila, after Frazier could no longer see Ali's right hand coming after the 14th round

CORRUPTION

"I broke the syndicate. I challenged them at a meeting. I said any man who thinks they have a grievance against me, let them stand up and face me on the floor. The president of the guild, who was a member of the syndicate, was angry because nobody stood up to back up the charges they were floating around about me. There were two or three stand-up guys who came to my assistance. I said I appreciate you fellows coming and offering me help, but I knew I was going to win. I knew everybody in there and I knew what their capabilities were and there wasn't nobody that I thought was going to do anything to me that I didn't want done. Six years later I got an award from the guild."

GREATNESS

"No matter how great you are, there is always somebody who can beat you."

Knowledge

"Marlon, I've taught you all you know, but I haven't taught you all I know."

—Admonishing welterweight champion Marlon Starling for not listening during a training session

Money

"When Ali was still in exile, he would go round to various gyms with his gear and find heavyweights to spar with. I had a young fighter named Ken Norton that didn't have too much experience, but I had taught him how to handle himself, and a sparring session he had with Ali had turned into a war. The session ended with Norton hitting Ali with a right hand counter-punch that had the crowd in the gym buzzing. Ali packed up his gear and left. The next day he came back and said he wanted Norton again. I told Norton not to put his stuff on. I said to Ali, 'Yesterday you came in here looking for a workout. Today you are here looking for a fight. When this kid fights you, he's gonna get paid for it.'"

Perspective

"I am in boxing but not of boxing."

Practice

"The way you train is the way you fight. You'll subconsciously make the moves you make in the gym, because they are the most recent things that are firmly embedded in your subconscious, and spots where they don't need to come out, they're going to come out."

PRESSURE

"You have to remain cool and collected in there. You have to think of anything you can to win, anything you can do to pull it out or protect your man."

PROFESSIONALS

"I don't give too much credence to what a fighter does as an amateur. Look at Henry Tillman. He beat Mike Tyson twice as an amateur, but as a pro look what happened. It's a world of difference. Those amateur fights are three rounds. When you're in a 10 or 12 round title fight, what is really inside of you comes out. Everything you've got gets tested."

"Alexis Arguello was the consumate professional. He was so thorough. He was meticulous in his execution. Deliberate, very deliberate. Everything he did, he prepared for."

RELATIONSHIPS

"I don't trust myself with a fighter I don't like. I'd be afraid that things other than good judgement would motivate me."

STRATEGY

"I charted Ali's strengths, the things he was a master at, and I also charted the things that he couldn't do. So I set up our strategy to avoid his strengths as much as we possibly could and to exploit his weaknesses as much as we possibly could.

One of them was that he could not throw the right hand uppercut properly. So we had Joe bob and weave in a more exaggerated way, just a little lower than he normally did, and stay in close, so Joe could work the body, and to watch for Ali's right hand drop to throw the uppercut. I told Joe the minute you see his right hand come down you throw the left hook. He's got nothing up there. The only time you could hit Ali was when he was punching. When he threw the uppercut, I told Joe to throw the hook. And that's the punch that hurt Ali so badly in the 11th round and the one that knocked him down in the 15th round. Ali was throwing the uppercut and Joe threw the hook."

TEACHING

"When I came along, there was a lot of jealousy. The old guys didn't want to impart their secrets. But I always felt what was good for boxing was good for me."

TRAINERS

"There are too many people walking up the street who put a towel over their shoulder and tell a kid they know what they're doing."

WORKING

"If I don't keep moving, maybe something will catch up to me."

—*Talking about training fighters into his 80s*

GOALS

"Try not to do too many things at once. Know what you want, the number one thing today and tomorrow. Persevere and get it done."

—NFL coach George Allen

"If you're bored with life—you don't get up every morning with a burning desire to do things—you don't have enough goals."

—Football coach Lou Holtz

"All winning teams are goal-oriented. Teams like these win consistently because everyone connected with them concentrates on specific objectives. They go about their business with blinders on; nothing will distract them from achieving their aims."

—Football coach Lou Holtz

"There's nothing wrong with setting goals, but it doesn't mean a thing if you don't pay attention to the day-to-day details."

—Football coach Don Shula

"The goal is too small and the goalies are too big."

—Hockey coach Scotty Bowman on why
goals are tough to score in the NHL

GREATNESS

"I name Wagner first on my list, not only because he was a great batting champion and base-runner, and also baseball's foremost shortstop, but because Honus could have been first at any other position, with the possible exception of pitcher. In all my career, I never saw such a versatile player."

—New York Giants manager John McGraw's
admiration of Honus Wagner

"The street to obscurity is paved with athletes who perform great feats before friendly crowds. Greatness in major league sports is the ability to win in a stadium filled with people who are pulling for you to lose."

—Football coach George Allen

"No club that wins a pennant once is an outstanding club. One which bunches two pennants is a good club. But a team which can win three in a row really achieves greatness."

—New York Giants baseball manager John McGraw

"The big trouble is not really who isn't in the Hall of Fame, but who is. It was established for a select few."

—Baseball manager Roger Hornsby

GOLF

"I don't want to play golf. When I hit a ball, I want someone else to go chase it."

—Baseball manager Roger Hornsby

HOCKEY

"You know a guy has a broken wrist, you hammer him there a few times and you don't have much trouble with him for the rest of the night. It's nothing personal."

—Hockey coach Punch Imlach

"Hockey is not just getting points and skating like some figure skater. Hitting is skill, body checking is a great skill, back checking is a great skill. And—I know people hate fighting—but fighting is a skill."

—Hockey coach and commentator Don Cherry

"If you keep the opposition on their asses, they don't score goals."

—Hockey coach Fred Shero

"You have to know what pro hockey is all about. You have to live and breathe and sleep it. You have to lose a few teeth and take some shots to the face. It's not a pretty thing."

—Hockey coach Ted Nolan

"That game tonight, Winnipeg, nothing but Swedes and Finns, a tea party, no hitting, nothing."

>*—Hockey coach and commentator Don Cherry talking about the playing style of European players*

HOME FIELD

"Maybe the other teams don't like to play here. Maybe they get spoiled by all the other new parks and they come here and get depressed."

>*—New York Mets manager Bobby Valentine, on why his team had such a good home record at Shea Stadium*

HOME RUNS

"The home run became glorified with Babe Ruth. Starting with him, batters have been thinking in terms of how far they could hit the ball, not how often."

>*—Manager Roger Hornsby on the popularity of the home run in baseball*

HONESTY

"When you get what you want in your struggle for self
And the world makes you king for a day
Just go to a mirror and look at yourself
And see what that man has to say
For it isn't your father, mother or wife
Whose judgment upon you must pass

The fellow whose verdict counts most in your life
Is the one staring back from the glass
Some people may think you're a straight-shootin' chum
And call you a wonderful guy
But the man in the glass says you're only a bum
If you can't look him straight in the eye
He's the fellow to please, never mind all the rest
For he's with you clear up to the end
And you've passed your most dangerous, difficult test
If the man in the glass is your friend
You may fool the whole world down the pathway of life
And get pats on the back as you pass
But your final reward will be heartaches and tears
If you've cheated the man in the glass."

*—The poem football coach Bill Parcells read to his
players before one of his retirements*

Humor

"The problem with having a sense of humor is often that
people you use it on aren't in a very good mood."

—Football coach Lou Holtz

Hustle

"I hustled on everything I hit."

*—Manager John McGraw on how
he once batted .424 as a player*

"Good things happen to those who hustle."

—Football coach Chuck Noll

"What you lack in talent can be made up with desire, hustle, and giving 110 percent all the time."

—Manager Don Zimmer

IGNORANCE

"These are two things I don't want to know, how they make hot dogs and what goes on in the NHL office."

—*Hockey coach Roger Neilson*

INDIVIDUALISTS

"Only in baseball can a team player be a pure individualist first and a team player second, within the rules and spirit of the game."

—*Baseball manager and general manager Branch Rickey*

INJURIES

"One player was lost because he broke his nose. How do you go about getting a nose in condition for football?"

—*Texas coach Darrell Royal, reacting to the number of injuries on one of his Longhorn teams*

"I'm going to send the injured reserve players out for the toss next time."

—NFL coach Mike McCormack, after one of his players, Baltimore Colts guard Robert Pratt, pulled a hamstring running on the field for the coin toss

"We've got more MRIs than RBIs on this team."

—Cincinnati Reds manager Jack McKeon on his team's injuries

"I called Blue Cross, but they hung up when they found out who it was."

—Cleveland Cavaliers basketball coach Bill Fitch on his team's many injuries

INTELLIGENCE

"They gave me a standing observation."

—Florida State University football coach Bill Peterson at the reaction he received at a banquet

"Mike Andrews's limits are limitless."

—Philadelphia Phillies manager Danny Ozark, talking about the limited, limitless potential of one of his players, Mike Andrews

"The more your players have to think on the basketball court, the slower their feet get."

—Basketball coach Jerry Tarkanian

"I know the Virginia players are smart because you need a 1,500 SAT to get in. I have to drop bread crumbs to get our players to and from class."

—George Raveling, the basketball coach at Washington State, comparing the intelligence of his players to that of his opponent, the University of Virginia

"Open up a ballplayer's head and you know what you'll find? A lot of little broads and a jazz band."

—Detroit Tigers manager Mayo Smith

"Lead us in a few words of silent prayer."

—Florida State University football coach Bill Peterson

"Slow thinkers are part of the game too. Some of these slow thinkers can hit a ball a long way."

—Baseball manager Alvin Dark

"Not only is he ambidextrous, but he can throw with either hand."

—Former college football coach and television analyst Duffy Daugherty

"We're not giving away any football players who could hurt us later. I don't mind people thinking I'm stupid, but I don't want to give them any proof."

—Houston Oilers coach Bum Phillips on trading players

"Son, looks to me like you're spending too much time on one subject."

—Texas A&M basketball coach Shelby Metcalf, after one of his players reported he had four Fs and one D

"Men, I want you just thinking of one word all season. One word and one word only: Super Bowl."

—Houston Oilers coach Bill Peterson, defining the goals of his team to just one word—or two

"He passed the bar exam, and there were times when I hardly passed a bar."

—Pittsburgh Pirates manager Jim Leyland on the difference between him and his friend, baseball manager Tony LaRussa, who is also an attorney

"It's better to be quiet and ignorant than to open your mouth and remove all doubt."

—Baseball manager John McNamara

"You guys line up alphabetically by height."

—Football coach Bill Peterson

"I don't care what the tape says. I didn't say it."

—Los Angeles Rams coach Ray Malavasi

"Tom."

—Houston Rockets basketball coach Tom Nissalke, when asked how he pronounced his name after being introduced as the team's new coach

INTENSITY

"Some guys are admired for coming to play, as the saying goes. I prefer those who come to kill."

—Baseball manager Leo Durocher on the intensity he likes to see in ballplayers

"That [Joe] Medwick never lost a debate in his life, mostly because he didn't bother. He was a one-man rampage."

—Baseball manager Leo Durocher on the intensity of outfielder Joe Medwick

Jobs

"If you don't win, you're going to be fired. If you do win, you've only put off the day you're going to be fired."

—Baseball manager Leo Durocher

"There are only two kinds of coaches: those who have been fired and those who are going to get fired."

—Houston Oilers coach Bum Phillips

"You can't keep on trading foot soldiers; sooner or later, the general's got to go."

—Hockey coach Pat Burns

"I get fired because I'm not a yes-man. The world's full of yes-men. The first year that I became manager, 1969, with the Twins, I won a division championship. And got fired. The Tigers hired me. I had made $35,000 and the Tigers gave me a big raise. I won another division title and got fired again. Texas hired me, and with a bigger raise. I came in second, and got fired. The Yankees hired me, and tripled my salary. When I got fired there, and Oakland hired me—they gave me an unbelievable raise. I've got a long-term contract now, but if I get fired again, I might run for president."

—Baseball manager Billy Martin on
his track record for being fired

"The only real way to know you've been fired is when you arrive at the ballpark and find your name has been scratched from the parking list."

—Baseball manager Billy Martin on how to
determine if you still have a job

"In order to become a big-league manager you have to be in the right place at the right time. That's rule number one."

—Baseball manager Leo Durocher
on finding managing jobs

"Mike Keenan has been responsible for creating a lot of good things for coaches, like mid-season job openings."

—Vancouver hockey coach Mark Crawford
on often-fired coach Mike Keenan

"Either they are going to accept what we ask them to do or they won't and they'll have to fire the coach. That's how it works."

—Hockey coach Mike Keenan when asked what would
happen if players didn't buy into his style of coaching

"All I know is, I pass people on the street these days, and they don't know whether to say hello or to say goodbye."

—Baseball manager Bill Martin
on his uncertain job status

"This is my third time. They say you're not a coach in the league 'till you've been fired. I must be getting pretty good."

—*Hockey coach Terry Simpson*
after being fired in Winnipeg

"The team overachieved all year. Everybody had career years. That may not happen again next year and guess whose fault it will be? Mine. So I want a two-year contract."

—*Cincinnati Reds manager Jack McKeon*

"So what, we're down 3-0. You know, if we lose on Tuesday, I don't believe a firing squad is going to show up at my house and put me down...although the last three or four coaches who have lost in the finals have been fired."

—*Washington Capitals hockey coach Ron Wilson*
when his team was down 3-0 to the Detroit
Red Wings in the 1998 Stanley Cup finals

The Herald-Times (Bloomington, Ind.)

BOBBY KNIGHT

I f there was ever a quotable coach, it is Bobby Knight. He has used words like weapons to lash out at his critics, and also as tools to build up his players to become winners. He, perhaps more than any other coach we have ever seen, has never been shy about speaking his mind, and so the media that he has despised throughout his career hangs on his every word.

Bobby Knight was born on October 25, 1940 in Massillon, Ohio. He was a star athlete, an all-state basketball player who was MVP of the Orville High School team in 1958. The 6-foot 5-inch Knight would go on to play at Ohio State University on the legendary team with Jerry Lucas that would win the NCAA national championship in 1960.

Knight began his coaching career as an assistant at Cuyahoga Falls High School in Ohio in 1962 and spent two years there before getting the opportunity to be part of the basketball staff at West Point as an assistant with the U.S. Military Academy from 1963 to 1965. That opportunity evolved into a head coaching job at Army at the age of 24—the youngest varsity coach in major college history—and he led the program from 1965 to 1971, building a strong program that would have the Knight signature defensive and disciplined style. He compiled a record of 102-50, and his Army teams led the nation in team defense for three consecutive seasons. They would play in four NIT tournaments in five seasons.

Then the Bobby Knight era began at Indiana University in 1971, and college basketball would never be the same. He established a legacy of excellence with his hard-nosed style and became an icon in that midwestern state that loves basketball. His Indiana teams won three NCAA championships (1976 [the 32-0 undefeated season], 1981, and 1987); played in five Final Fours; won one NIT title (1979); and 11 Big Ten Conference championships.

Knight was named national Coach of the Year four times and Big Ten Coach of the Year five times. He took his winning ways to the international stage, and won the Pan American gold medal in 1979 and the Olympic gold medal in 1984. In fact, the gold medal win made Knight one of three coaches to ever win an NCAA championship, and NIT title, and an Olympic gold medal. He was also one of two coaches to both play and coach on a national championship team, the other being Dean Smith. He was the youngest coach to reach 200, 300, and 400 victories.

But this success was always marred by Knight's volatile temper and his outrageous statements. An arrest warrant was issued for him in Puerto Rico after he got into an argument with a police officer. He threw chairs during games and insulted officials, athletic directors, and any others who dared to question his methods. Toward the end of his tenure in Indiana, he was consistently on the brink of losing his job for his antics, until finally, after a tape surfaced of him physically abusing one of his players, Neil Reed, during a practice, the end was at hand. Knight was put on probation, but it didn't last long because he got into an argument with a nasty student on campus and was fired. Knight would quickly find another job, hired as head coach at Texas Tech University in 2001, and had immediate success, posting a 23-10 record, with a career mark of 786-299. Knight was inducted into the Basketball Hall of Fame in 1991.

Bobby Knight on:

Alumni

"You know, I wish all alumni would be canonized. That way we coaches would only have to kiss your rings."

Anger

"There are times when my passion for basketball led me into confrontations that I could have handled a lot better. I've always been too confrontational, especially when I know I'm right."

"Sure I have a temper. But I don't think that's bad. It's when a temper controls the person, instead of the person controlling the temper, that I think a problem exists."

"Christ had a temper. Christ destroyed the tables in the temple, so when you start talking about people who have a temper, I think you have to start there. Don't misunderstand me. I'm not trying to draw any parallels between myself and Christ."

"President Myles Brand, in a meeting with me, gave me a set of guidelines he expects me to follow if I want to continue as Indiana University's basketball coach. I have absolutely no problem with the guidelines. The establishment of effective and proper guidelines can, in the long run, help me become a better coach. As I have said before, I recognize that I have a problem with my temper. For those times my situation has ever caused me to do anything to give anyone understandable and testifiable reason to be upset, I am sincerely sorry."

—Prepared statement after a meeting with Brand when he was nearly fired

ATTITUDE

"You are never going to be driven anywhere worthwhile, but you sure as hell drive yourself to a lot of great places. It is up to you to drive yourself there."

BASKETBALL

"You don't play against opponents, you play against the game of basketball."

"There isn't anything, except for my family, that I think about more than I do basketball."

"I think basketball is fun for me because I haven't changed very much. I think some people don't feel that it is, because they've had to change with the times, you know, and I'm almost obsolete and way behind the times."

"Basketball is American, it's hot dogs, popcorn, and 'The Star Spangled Banner.'"

CHAMPIONSHIPS

"People want national championship banners. People want to talk about Indiana being competitive. How do we get there? We don't get there with milk and cookies."

CHEATING

"If my primary purpose here at Indiana is to go out and win ballgames, I can probably do that as well as anybody can. I would just cheat, get some money from a lot of people around Indianapolis who want to run the operation that way, and just go out and get the best basketball players I can. Then we'd beat everybody all the time."

COACHING

"If you're a coach you're going to get your ass beat now and then."

"I would rather be thought of as a teacher than a coach."

"There's probably nobody that's ever coached basketball that just likes the game any better than I do. I mean I really like the game."

CRITICS

"When my time on Earth is gone
And my activities here are past
I want that they should bury me upside down
So my critics can kiss my ass."

—Speaking at the 1994 senior day ceremonies.

"I fortunately have never worried about irritating people."

"I stood up, unzipped my pants, lowered my shorts, and placed my bare ass on the window. That's the last thing I wanted those people to see of me."

—Talking about how he left Puerto Rico in 1979 after getting into a legal dispute with a police officer there

"I can't tell you, and I don't even like discussing it, the number of times I've gone home and said, 'God, I wish I hadn't gotten on that kid like that.' I wish I didn't think I had to get on him. Hey, I'm not—I never once said I'm perfect. I have made mistakes, but that really doesn't separate me from anyone else. Am I susceptible or liable to criticism? Certainly, and sometimes fairly."

"I once told a guy I would like to have carved on my tombstone, 'He was honest, and he didn't kiss anybody's ass.'"

"I have often said this to some sanctimonious self-righteous critics that I have: 'I would hope that when judgment day comes, they don't appear before St. Peter's table with me, and only one space available for both of us, and the judgment being made on who has done the most for fellow man. I have no doubt St. Peter will turn to me and say, 'Robert, pass through the gate.'"

DESIRE

"Failure, to me, is not having the desire to try. Having the desire to try is in its own way success."

DISCIPLINE

"Discipline is doing what you have to do, and doing it as well as you possibly can, and doing it that way all the time."

"I think it suffices to say that no matter what you're doing, whether it be playing defense or the fast break, discipline is a matter of making the proper choice of what to do at the proper time."

DRUGS

"I don't feel sorry for Len Bias....[He] was better than anyone in this room...but he's dead. He's not sick, he's not hurt, he's dead....He wanted to be one of the boys. He wanted to be cool. Well he was so cool, he's cold. He's cold as heck."

GOD

"God couldn't care less if we win or not. He is not going to parachute in through the roof of this building and score when we need points."

HUMAN NATURE

"Your biggest opponent isn't the other guy. It's human nature."

INDIANA

"Basketball may have been invented in Massachusetts, but it was made for Indiana."

"I couldn't have picked anyplace as well-suited for me as Indiana."

LAW

"F--- 'em, f--- 'em all. I'll tell you what, their basketball is a hell of a lot easier to beat than their court system. The only G-------- thing they know how to do is grow bananas."

—Speaking about his legal problems
in Puerto Rico in 1979

MOTIVATION

"We put his dick in a vise. I twisted it. We stuck a red-hot poker up his ass and poured hot water down his mouth and I told him if he promised to play well, we'd quit all that."

—Talking about how he got a player to
perform so well in a particular game

"I have never been one to hesitate to get on people, and maybe sometimes I get on kids a little too much."

"A motivator isn't always the guy who just pats you on the ass. He's the guy who kicks you in the ass occasionally."

"Right here is the key to success in coaching. Probably no motivational device I've ever come across is as good as this."

"I've done close to a thousand things to motivate kids as individuals or teams. And I'll guarantee a lot of them I wouldn't want to talk about at a church social, PTA meeting, or garden party. But we're not teaching kids how to play canasta."

—On his habit of holding up a bullwhip

REFEREES

"The most susceptible guy in any gambling scheme is an official, without any question. I mean, if we only knew the truth about games that were controlled by officials having gambling interests, I think it would be amazing."

"Bad officiating has almost ruined the basketball in this league."

"I don't think there's an official in the country who knows as much about basketball as I do. Not even close. Or as much as any other coach knows."

PLAYERS

"An Indiana player has the enthusiasm of an evangelist, the discipline of a monk, and the heart of a warrior who never loses the honesty and character of a small boy."

"I tell them that wherever you start in life there will be others above you. Get used to it now."

"A player enters the Hall of Fame on his ability. A coach enters on the ability of his players."

"Recruit jackasses, and they play like jackasses."

"I want a persistent player, not the consistent player. I want a team that is persistent, unyielding, enduring, staying with something despite obstacles."

"If [Iowa coach Steve] Alford wants to sit down and talk with me, instead of holding press conferences and talking about a bunch of s---, I'll explain things to him."

—*Speaking of former player Steve Alford and the estrangement between the two*

"If there are any problems with Keith Smart, you are going to see his ass on the bench. That's the way we handle ego at Indiana. You see the bench gives your ass a message, then your ass gives your brain a message, and then your brain will probably get Keith Smart to play a helluva lot better."

—*Talking about one of his star players, Keith Smart*

"If my reaction to the jeering from the stands on Tuesday night offended any true Hoosier fans, I am deeply sorry and wish to apologize. I realize that you have not always agreed with what I have done or said. I probably wouldn't agree with all you have said or did, either. P.S. We have been working on Patrick's passing."

—Reaction after he kicked his son,
Patrick, at a 1993 home game

"We are going to redshirt Patrick [Knight] next year so he'll have me as a coach for 5 years. When Patrick is done, having me as a father and a coach, Patrick Knight will undoubtedly have the most blistered ass in the history of basketball."

"I'm not sure that an athlete is prepared to be a role model. He has a lot of attention paid to him that he shouldn't have, and then the athletes tend to think of themselves as better than they are."

PREPARATION

"Most people have the will to win, few have the will to prepare to win."

"The will to succeed is important, but what's more important is the will to prepare."

"The hardest part of my job is waiting to play, the final preparation. Once the game starts, I'm fine."

SPORTSWRITERS

"All of us learn to write in the second grade. Most of us go on to greater things."

"A coach flies off the handle in public and everyone sees him. I'd like to be around to see what one of you guys does when somebody changes your copy."

"For me to get an award from the press, I know there's been no favoritism."

—Reacting to being named Associated Press Coach of the Year in 1989

"God damn, there are a lot of you guys I'd like to see get fired. What the hell makes you think I'm going to save you? From the Christian depths of my heart, I'll do what's necessary. So ask your question."

—Answering a question from a reporter at a press conference who said he would be fired if he didn't ask it to Knight

STUPIDITY

"I do dumb things sometimes."

"I don't always have to wait until the next morning to regret something I did that was kinda dumb."

STUDENTS

"I've got a little class I teach. There are a lot of you who wouldn't like my class. I won't let you come in barefooted. You can't wear a hat. If you cut class, it's an automatic C. And if you cut it twice, you'd better have time to go to Drop and Add."

SUCCESS

"Practice structure determines success."

WINNING

"Victory has never been a particularly satisfying thing to me. It's really hard for me to say, 'Well, we won.'"

LEADERSHIP

"Leadership starts at the top."

—DeMatha High School basketball coach
Morgan Wooten

"Leadership is what develops when each man is an extension of the other."

—Football coach Bill Walsh

LEARNING

"I never learn anything talking. I only learn things when I ask questions."

—Football coach Lou Holtz

LEISURE

"Leisure is the handmaiden of the devil."

—Baseball manager and general manager Branch Rickey

LIFE

"You're born with two strikes against you, so don't take a third one on your own."

>—*Philadelphia Athletics owner and manager*
>*Connie Mack on his philosophy of life*

"Life is 10 percent what happens to me and 90 percent how I react to it."

>—*Football coach Lou Holtz*

"Life is a game, and it's the greatest game of all time."

>—*Football coach Joe Gibbs*

LOSING

"On my tombstone just write, 'The sorest loser that ever lived."

>—*Baseball manager Earl Weaver*

"Every time you win, you're reborn. When you lose, you die a little."

>—*NFL coach George Allen on the pain of losing*

"The way we have been playing, I might tell my players not to cross the picket line."

>—*Baseball manager Whitey Herzog, when faced with the prospects of a strike during the 1979 season*

"We're the only team in history that could lose nine games in a row and then go into a slump."

>—*Cleveland Cavaliers basketball coach Bill Fitch*

"Frankly, I'm in favor of it."

>—*NFL coach John McKay being questioned on the execution on the field of his Tampa Bay Bucs squad*

"Show me a good loser in professional sports, and I'll show you an idiot."

—Baseball manager Leo Durocher

"When you win, say nothing. When you lose, say less."

—NFL coach and owner Paul Brown

"There was never a champion who, to himself, was a good loser. There's a vast difference between a good sport and a good loser."

—Football coach Red Blaik

"If anybody is writing that this is a nice, rosy situation, they're on drugs. And if we believe it, than we are taking even better drugs."

—Chicago Blackhawk hockey coach Craig Hartsburg
on his team's poor start in the season

"We need three kinds of pitching: left handed, right handed, and relief."

—Baseball manager Whitey Herzog
on his team's poor pitching

"Finish last in your league and they call you an idiot. Finish last in medical school and they call you a doctor."

—Basketball coach Abe Lemons

"I've taken this team as far as I can."

—Women's basketball coach Lynn Wheeler after resigning
from Iowa State after 14 straight losses

"We're so bad right now that, for us, back-to-back home runs means one today and another one tomorrow."

—Baseball manager Earl Weaver

"I don't apologize for anything. When I make a mistake, I take the blame and go on from there. I just despise to lose, and that has taken a man of mediocre ability and made a pretty good coach out of him."

—*Football coach Woody Hayes*

"Even Napoleon had his Watergate."

—*Philadelphia Phillies manager Danny Ozark on his team blowing a 15-game lead*

"At Arkansas, they made a stamp to commemorate you. Then, after last year, they had to stop making it because people were spitting on the wrong side."

—*Football coach Lou Holtz*

"Nice guys finish last."

—*Baseball manager Leo Durocher*

"It wasn't as easy as you think. It's hard to stay awake that long."

—*Whitworth College football coach Hugh Campbell after his team won a game 70-30*

"The only difference between this and Custer's last stand was Custer didn't have to look at the tape afterwards."

—*Tampa Bay hockey coach Terry Crisp after a 10-0 loss*

"All quitters are good losers."

—*Football coach Bob Zuppke*

"If I am the problem, I can be removed."

—*Basketball coach Doug Collins after his Detroit Pistons lost 11 of their first 15 games*

"Maybe we tired them out tonight and they won't come out and swing the bats tomorrow."

—*Baseball manager Lou Piniella, on his Seattle Mariners 17-2 loss to the Cleveland Indians in an American League Division Series game*

"I feel sorry for the fans. You pay that much money to see a game, you expect professional play. We walked 14 people today. We pitched like a bunch of 12-year-olds. We had a guy get picked off when we're six runs down. If you want any more stories, go out in the clubhouse. They're the ones making all the money. Have them explain how they did and how they performed in front of 47,000 people."

—*Baltimore Orioles owner manager Ray Miller, talking to reporters after an 11-10 Orioles loss put their early season 1999 record at 4-14*

"I went to church the other day to pray for our pitchers, but there weren't enough candles."

—*Cincinnati Reds manager Jack McKeon*

"Last season we couldn't win at home, and this season we can't win on the road. My failure as a coach is that I can't think of any place else to play."

—*Vancouver hockey coach Harry Neale*

"I knew we were in for a long season when we lined up for the national anthem on opening day and one of my players said, 'Every time I hear that song I have a bad game.'"

—*Baseball manager Jim Leyland*

"About a year and a half or so after the World Series, a guy asked me how long it took me to get over that last game. I told him, 'As soon as it happens, I'll let you know.'"

—*Cleveland Indians manager Mike Hargrove talking about the pain of his team losing the seventh game of the 1997 World Series to the Florida Marlins in the 11th inning*

"What you get from games you lose is extremely important."

—*Basketball coach Pat Riley*

"You know that saying that you learn more from defeats than victories? Then we're going to become Einsteins. We're going to be rocket scientists. We're going to find a cure for cancer."

—*Florida Marlins manager John Boles*
on his team's dismal prospects

"When coaches don't want to talk, they say you don't understand. It's funny how fans and media understand wins. But everyone gets stupid with losses. Losing breeds stupidity."

—*Football coach and sportscaster John Madden*

"If you can accept defeat and open your pay envelope without feeling guilty, you're stealing."

—*Football coach George Alien*

"I'd rather be a football coach. That way you only lose 11 games a year."

—*Basketball coach Abe Lemons*

"If there is such a thing as a good loser, then the game is crooked."

—*Baseball manager Billy Martin*

"No one's gonna give a damn in July if you lost a game in March."

—*Baseball manager Earl Weaver*

LUCK

"Luck? If the roof fell in and Diz [Dean] was sitting in the middle of the room, everybody else would be buried and a gumdrop would fall in his mouth."

—*Baseball manager Leo Durocher*
on the good fortune of pitcher Dizzy Dean

"Luck is what happens when preparation meets opportunity."

—*Texas football coach Darrel Royal*

Texas Sports Hall of Fame, Waco Tex.

TOM LANDRY

Tom Landry became known as the personification of perfection and efficiency, but it came with the cost of his reputation as a cold, humorless, football coach. But he was not perfect, and he was not cold. He was a man who placed a high value on dignity, and that came through in his words throughout his successful career coaching the Dallas Cowboys.

Thomas Wade Landry was born September 11, 1924, in Mission, Texas, deep in the Rio Grande Valley. He was a star football player at Mission High School, and went on to play football at the University of Texas. However, Landry left school after one semester to join the U.S. Army Air Corps. He became a decorated fighter pilot in World War II, flying 30 combat missions. His older brother Robert died as a fighter pilot in the war.

After the war, Landry went back to the University of Texas, where he was a standout back. He would go on to play as a defensive back for the New York Giants, and his ability to read offenses and create defenses on the field landed him a position as player-coach at the age of 29, in charge of the Giants defense. It was there that Landry developed his 4-3 defense, changing the 5-2 that had been there and creating what was to become the middle linebacker position. It revolutionized defensive football, as Landry did throughout his career, both on offense (with the multiple offense) and defense.

Tex Schram hired Landry in 1960 as the first head coach of the new NFL franchise in Dallas, the Cowboys, and the coach went through some difficult early years, with a 13-38-3 record after four seasons, including an 0-11-1 record his first year as head coach. But he stuck to his vision, and would build the Cowboys into a perennial winner and the class of the league. They made the playoffs for the first time in 1967 against the Green Bay Packers, losing 34-27. The following season they would play the Packers in the infamous "Ice Bowl" playoff game in Green Bay, with a negative 40 wind chill, losing 17-14 on the Bart Starr quarterback sneak over guard Jerry Kramer.

Landry's team reached the Super Bowl for the first time in 1971, losing in the last minute to the Baltimore Colts on a Jim O'Brien field goal. But Landry continued to drive the Cowboys to success, even after each difficult postseason loss, and it paid off the following season, when the Cowboys defeated the Miami Dolphins 24-3 in the Super Bowl to win the first of two NFL championships under Landry. The second came in 1977 in a win over the Denver Broncos. Before Landry was done, he had put together a championship legacy: two Super Bowl wins, five NFC championships, and 13 division titles, with a remarkable string of 20 straight winning seasons.

It didn't end well for Landry. The Cowboys fell on hard times, and in his final season they went a dismal 3-13. New owner Jerry Jones unceremoniously fired him in 1989, after 270 wins, 179 losses, and six ties as the Cowboys head coach for 29 seasons.

There was a public outcry at the way Landry—forever identified for walking the sidelines wearing his famous fedora—was treated at the end, and those who had criticized him for being a cold person now saw him as a sympathetic figure. But he handled his situation with the same dignity that he carried with him to the very end, when he passed away at the age of 75 in 2000. Before he died, Landry was inducted into the Pro Football Hall of Fame and the team's Ring of Honor, where he belonged, because he was a man of honor, and his words were proof of that.

TOM LANDRY ON:

CHARACTER

"You don't build character without somebody slapping you around. We got to the point where we thought we could take it easy and win. Why even my wife was talking of an undefeated season. That's sure sign of death...I'll tell you this, we'll be a different team next week."

—After an unexpected loss

"People striving, being knocked down and coming back, that's what builds character. I've seen very little character in players who never had to face adversity."

"A team that has character doesn't need stimulation."

COACHING

"Perhaps the toughest call for a coach is weighing what is best for an individual against what is best for the team. Keeping a player on the roster just because I liked him personally, or even because of his great contributions to the team in the past, when I felt some one else could do more for the team, would be a disservice to the team's goals."

"I can't believe that call, the sneak. It wasn't a good call. But now, it's a great call."

—Reacting to the quarterback sneak by Bart Starr with 13 seconds to give the Green Bay Packers a 21-17 win over Dallas in the NFL championship game, now known as the "Ice Bowl"

CONCENTRATION

"I don't believe you can be emotional and concentrate the way you should to be effective. As a team, we win by concentrating, by thinking. The players don't want to see me rushing around and screaming. They want to believe I know what I'm doing."

CONFIDENCE

"It is hard to put your finger on why you make the decision that you make, I'm a great believer in my own convictions, but I pray a great deal that I'll make the right decision. I have no doubt that there is something other than himself that leads man."

COWBOYS

"America's team. The moment I heard it I thought, 'Oh, no, everybody's really going to be gunning for us now.' I don't know anyone on the Cowboys who liked the label to start with. So many newspapers picked up on it that other teams used it as a motivational tool against us. However, what seemed so presumptuous at first eventually became part of the proud Cowboys's tradition."

"I'll be with you in spirit always."

—*Speaking to his team in his last meeting before leaving*

DISCIPLINE

"Most successful players not only accept rules and limitations, I believe they need them. In fact, I believe players are free to perform at their best only when they know what the expectations are and where the limits stand."

FOOTBALL

"Football is an incredible game. Sometimes it's so incredible, it's unbelievable."

GOALS

"Setting a goal is not the main thing. It is deciding how you will go about achieving it and staying with that plan."

GOD

"God doesn't interfere. We have great Christian friends around the league. He just gives you the courage to excel, the confidence to perform to the best of your ability."

LEADERSHIP

"Leadership is getting someone to do what they don't want to do, to achieve what they want to achieve."

"Leadership is a matter of having people look at you and gain confidence, seeing how you react. If you're in control, they're in control."

"A successful leader has to be innovative. If you're not one step ahead of the crowd, you'll soon be a step behind everyone else."

LEGACY

"People will forget me quick."

—On his firing from the Cowboys

LIFE

"Today, you have 100 percent of your life left."

"First become a winner in life. Then it's easier to become a winner on the field."

LOSING

"I've learned that something constructive comes from every defeat."

MONEY

"Money has changed sports. It's just different. We didn't have that much money. That's what the big difference is. Just kind of ruins the whole thing. It's hard for the fans when players switch teams every year and entire franchises move. It's amazing how many people that I run into say that they're not really watching it anymore."

MOTIVATION

"I don't believe in team motivation. I believe in getting a team prepared so it knows it will have the necessary confidence when it steps on a field and be prepared to play a good game."

PLAYERS

"Here was one of the greatest running talents I'd ever seen come into professional football. What bothered me even more than his wasted talent was the fact that Duane [Thomas] was obviously a troubled young man. He needed help, and I hadn't been able to get through to him."

PREPARATION

"If you are prepared, you will be confident, and will do the job."

SUCCESS

"The more successful you become, the longer the yardstick people use to measure you by."

THE HAT

"My hats did give me an identity. In fact, if I had a dollar for every time someone has seen me bareheaded and said, 'I almost didn't recognize you without your hat on,' I could have bought the Cowboys myself."

TEAMWORK

"There's a misconception about teamwork. Teamwork is the ability to have different thoughts about things; it's the ability to argue and stand up and say loud and strong what you feel. But in the end, it's also the ability to adjust to what is the best for the team."

WEATHER

"I like the South because it is so much warmer on the sidelines than it is up North."

WINNING

"When you want to win a game, you have to teach. When you lose a game, you have to learn."

"A winner never stops trying."

WHAT OTHERS HAVE SAID ABOUT TOM LANDRY:

"If he was married to Raquel Welch, he'd expect her to cook."

—Cowboys quarterback Don Meredith

"I don't know. I only played there nine years."

—Cowboys fullback Walt Garrison, former Cowboy fullback, when asked if Landry ever smiled

"With all we learned from him, about football and life—being prepared—he was a huge impact, just a huge impact on thousands of young men."

—Cowboys defensive tackle Bob Lilly

"I just always thought that there was no team we could ever come up against that could be more prepared, better prepared, than we were."

—Cowboys running back Tony Dorsett

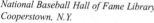

National Baseball Hall of Fame Library
Cooperstown, N.Y.

TOMMY LASORDA

One of the most sought after speakers in all of sports is former Los Angeles Dodgers baseball manager Tommy Lasorda. His positive motivational style of speaking and his ability to find the right words in tough times have made him one of the all-time quoted managers in all of baseball.

Born in 1927, Lasorda was a young pitcher who came up in the Dodgers organization. He was a successful minor league pitcher. Once, in a Class C 15-inning game in 1948, he struck out 25 batters. Lasorda would go on to compile a 98-49 record with Montreal in the International League, including an 18-6 record in 1958. But he was up against a tough major league pitching staff when he tried to break into the Dodgers roster, which included Don Newcombe, Preacher Roe, Sandy Koufax, and Don Drysdale. During his brief major league stints, Lasorda failed, posting an 0-4 record in 26 innings pitched. But his future was to be in the dugout, not on the mound.

Lasorda became a Dodger scout in 1961 and then a minor league manager in 1965. He won five pennants and finished second twice and third once through 1972, and was moved up after that to a coach on the Dodgers staff under the manager who he had played for briefly in Brooklyn, long-time Dodgers skipper, Walt Alston. At the end of the 1976 season, Alston retired, and Lasorda took over the job he seemed destined for: managing the Dodgers.

He had immediate success, managing the Dodgers to two straight National League pennants in 1977 and 1978—the first league manager to win pennants in his first two seasons—but lost to the New York Yankees both times in the World Series. However, Lasorda captured his first Major League World Championship and got a measure of revenge against the Yankees when the Dodgers won the 1981 World Series, defeating New York. His Dodgers teams won the NL West division title in 1983 and 1985, but lost in the NL Championship Series. Lasorda's finest moment, though, may have been when he managed the Dodgers to the 1988 World Championship, leading an underdog team to an upset win over the powerful Oakland A's, with a hurt Kirk Gibson coming off the bench in the bottom of the ninth inning to blast a pinch-hit, game-winning home run off previously untouchable reliever Dennis Eckersley that changed the entire series.

Lasorda would manage the Dodgers until June 1996, when he suffered a mild heart attack and underwent an angioplasty. One month later, he officially retired, with a managing record of 1,099-957, a League Championship mark of 16-14, and a record of 12-22 in World Series games. He has remained in the Dodgers front office since then.

Lasorda was so beloved in the game that the National Baseball Hall of Fame waived its five-year rule (having to have been retired from baseball for five years) and inducted Lasorda into the Hall of Fame in 1997. But he had one more managing job to do, and he was the perfect man for the job. In 2000, Lasorda took a group of minor league players and castoffs to the Olympics in Sydney and defeated the powerful Cuban team to capture the gold medal for the United States.

TOMMY LASORDA ON:

AGE

"The average age of our bench is deceased."

AUTOGRAPHS

"Always give an autograph when somebody asks you."

BASEBALL

"Baseball is like driving, it's the one who gets home safely that counts."

"Football, you got to be strong. Basketball, you got to be tall. But baseball, you can play it at all sizes and that's why it's America's game, because anyone can play it."

"I love doubleheaders. That way I get to keep my uniform on longer."

CALIFORNIA

"You're not legally dead until you lose your tan."

CHEATING

"No, we don't cheat. And even if we did, I'd never tell you."

EDUCATION

"Education can't be taken away from you. Your morals, your education are things they can't take away from you."

FANS

"Listen, if you start worrying about the people in the stands, before too long you're up in the stands with them."

HITTING

"My theory of hitting was just to watch the ball as it came in and hit it."

INJURIES

"I walk into the clubhouse and it's like walking into the Mayo Clinic. We have four doctors, three therapists, and five trainers. Back when I broke in, we had one trainer who carried a bottle of rubbing alcohol and by the seventh inning he had drunk it all."

MANAGING

"I believe managing is like holding a dove in your hand. If you hold it too tightly you kill it, but if you hold it too loosely, you lose it."

"I love my job. There's a saying in this country that any man or woman who loves their job has never worked a day in their life. I really love my job, so old man sickness and death gets tired of chasing me, cause he knows he don't stand a chance."

"My responsibility is to get my 25 guys playing for the name on the front of their uniform and not the one on the back."

Marriage

"Marriage is not easy. You have to have faith in each other and when times are tough, you have to stay closer."

"My wife accused me the other day of loving baseball more than I loved her. I told her she was right, but that I did love her more than football and basketball."

Money

"All last year we tried to teach him [Fernando Valenzuela] English, and the only word he learned was *million*."

—Talking about the language problems with pitcher Fernando Valenzuela and the money the young pitcher would be making

Motivation

"I motivate players through communication, being honest with them, having them respect and appreciate your ability and your help."

"The most important part of motivating players is telling them the truth, telling them what it's going to take for them to have to win, telling them to play for the name on the front of their shirt, not the one on the back of their shirt."

OLYMPICS

"I don't know who you are, where you come from, if you're good, mediocre, or bad, but I'm going to tell you something right now, when this thing is all over, the whole world is going to know you guys. You want to know why? Because you are coming to play your hearts out. You are coming for one thing, to bring the gold medal to the United States, where it belongs in baseball. Baseball is our game, and we cannot let these teams beat us. When you come here, you do not represent your family, nor the school you went to, or the town you come from, or the organization that signed you. You represent the United States of America, and you're going to do everything you can to make the United States proud of you and you're not going to do anything over here to embarrass our country."

> —*Recalling what he told the minor leaguers and castoffs who made up the 2000 Olympic baseball team that Lasorda managed to a gold medal*

"This was bigger than the World Series. This was bigger than the Dodgers. This was bigger than Major League Baseball. When we won World Championships, the Dodger fans were happy, but the San Francisco Giant fans weren't, nor were the San Diego Padres fans, nor the Cincinnati Reds fans. But when you win that gold medal, then the United States is happy."

> —*Talking about the impact of winning the gold medal*

Perspective

"Sometimes you might feel cheated, denied, or deprived. Just look over your shoulder to see how many people are worse off than you, and then you'll realize just how lucky you are."

Players

"There are three types of baseball players: those who make it happen, those who watch it happen, and those who wonder what happens."

"I remember my father—someone asked him, 'Which one of your five sons do you love best?' And I thought he would say me. But he held up his fingers and said, 'which one do I love best?' The same applies to my players."

—*Asked who his favorite player was he ever managed*

"It couldn't have happened to a greater guy. Well, yes it could. It could have happened to me."

—*Talking about pitcher Jerry Reuss's no-hitter*

"I knew June was Pedro [Guerrero]'s favorite month, so I told him that in the U.S., June had 60 days. I'd see him in July and say, 'Well, Pedro, it's June 52 and I see you're still hot.'"

—*After Pedro Guerrero hit 15 home runs in June*
and .460 in July

"There really is a Big Dodger in the sky and I think he has come down and taken over Hersheiser's body."

—*After pitcher Orel Hersheiser's eighth*
no-run game in 10 starts in 1988

PRAYER

"I wanted to go out a winner. I had 2 and 0, and I saw the manager with one foot on the dugout steps and I knew what that means, he was going to take me out. So I turned my back on the hitter and said, 'Dear God, please get me out of this jam. I want to win.' The manager said, 'Throw the ball.' I said, 'I'm talking to God!' 'Throw the ball!' So I threw the ball. And that hitter hit a line drive as hard as he could. And I thought it was a base hit, but third baseman leapt up and caught it, threw it to first base, and it was a triple play, and then I went on to win the game. It's a lesson to all of us that there's nothing wrong with praying and nothing wrong with asking God for help."

—Referring to his last game as a pitcher, when he walked three batters to load the bases, with no out, and went 2-0 on the fourth hitter

STRESS

"Guys ask me, don't I get burned out? How can you get burned out doing something you love? I ask you, have you ever got tired of kissing a pretty girl?"

SUCCESS

"The price of success can only come through the avenue of hard work. In order for you to be a success, you have to outwork your opponents. That's the only way we're going to succeed."

"About the only problem with success is that it does not teach you how to deal with failure."

THE DODGERS

"I bleed Dodger blue and when I die, I'm going to the big Dodger in the sky."

"Say 'Dodgers' and people know you're talking about baseball. Say 'Braves' and they ask, 'What reservation?' Say 'Reds' and they think of communism. Say 'Padres' and they look around for a priest."

"I say this from the bottom of my heart, that if you don't root for the Dodgers, you might not get into heaven."

UNDERDOGS

"When you're the underdog, that should inspire you all the more. That's what I did in '88, when we were the underdogs, and I told my guys we're going beat them. Think of David and Goliath and people were betting on Goliath and David won. And that's what we did when we beat the Mets, and then we played Oakland Athletics and we beat them. They had all the stars, Conseco, McGwire, Lansford, all these great players, and we beat them in a five-game World Series. Why? Because we wanted them more than they did. And coach, make those players understand: How bad do they want those fruits of victory?"

—*Referring to the Dodgers remarkable 1988 World Series upset win over the favored Oakland Athletics*

WHINING

"Eighty percent of the people who hear them [your troubles] don't care and the other 20 percent are glad you're having them."

WINNING

"When we win, I'm so happy I eat a lot. When we lose, I'm so depressed, I eat a lot. When we're rained out, I'm so disappointed I eat a lot."

•••

In 1998, Tommy Lasorda testified before the U.S. Senate Judiciary Committee, not on baseball matters, but on a resolution supporting an amendment to protect the American flag from acts of physical desecration. Here is that testimony:

"My name is Tommy Lasorda and I am the general manager of the Los Angeles Dodgers. Nearly five decades ago, I began living a dream as I embarked on a career that allowed me to be a part of the great American pastime as a major league player, coach, and manager for the world-famous Los Angeles Dodgers.

"Not only have I lived every school boy's dream, but I have also been present during a number of historic moments that have brought the country together in a way that few other events can.

"During the 1977 World Series, Reggie Jackson hit four towering home runs on four consecutive pitches to lead the enemy Yankees past my Dodgers for the World Championship.

"On September 28, 1988, Dodger great Orel Hershiser needed 10 scoreless innings to top the record for consecutive scoreless innings set in 1968 by Don Drysdale. Locked in a scoreless pitcher's duel with the San Diego Padres, sports fans from around the country tuned in to watch Hershiser break this long-standing record.

"In the first game of the 1988 World Series against the Oakland Athletics, I called upon injured Dodger Kirk Gibson to pinch-hit in the bottom of the ninth inning against the unhittable Dennis Eckersley. As many Americans remember, Gibson, in his only at-bat of the series, hit a home run to cap a dramatic come-from-behind win and propel us to a World Championship.

"As I look back at the American history I have been privileged enough to be a part of, I can't help thinking about the other part of our American pastime that holds us all together: the respect we show for each other, and the nation, when we take off our caps, face the American flag, and sing the national anthem before every major league game. For you see, baseball, like the American flag and national anthem, ties everyone in this great country of ours together.

"I am here today for a number of reasons. First, because I proudly served this great country in the Army's Special Service unit from 1946 to 1947. And because when I travel the country for the Dodgers and watch the news, I am reminded that one of the greatest things we can teach the children of tomorrow—respect for God and country—is getting more and more difficult to pass on.

"One of the best ways we can teach this respect is by protecting our flag from physical desecration. Too many Americans do not realize that the Supreme Court in 1989, by just one vote, declared that this behavior is protected "speech" under the First Amendment. Five judges took away the right of the people to protect their flag—a right exercised since our birth, defended by the Justices on five previous Supreme Courts, and by James Madison and Thomas Jefferson who helped adopt the first flag and write the First Amendment.

"Today, because of the Supreme Court's decision, the flag is just another piece of cloth that can be burned and soiled with impunity.

"In the rotunda of the state capital in Lansing, Michigan, a young man wiped his rear end with the American flag at the Governor's State of the State Address. The event was taped by the NBC affiliate as the crowd chanted, "What do we want? Revolution. When do we want it? Now." Police stood by and watched because the courts say this behavior is 'free speech.'

"In Wallingford, Connecticut, a young man burned American flags and poured red paint over a church's statue of the Virgin Mary, breaking off the thumb and cracking the upper portion of the monument.

"In Lafayette Square, just a few blocks from where we sit today, 2,000 angry protestors raised their voices against the Clinton administration's stand against Iraqi President Saddam Hussein by carry anti-war banners and burning the American flag.

"In a small Wisconsin town, a high school student pulled down the American flag from a golf course, defecated on it, and left it on the steps of the club house. The district attorney tried to prosecute the young man, but the judge threw it out because defecating on the flag is 'free speech.'

"Contrast these occurrences with one of the most heroic acts ever to take place on the field during a Major League Baseball game.

"On April 25, 1976, as we played the Chicago Cubs at Dodger Stadium, I witnessed a flag burning. In the middle of the fourth inning, as the fielders were warming up, two protestors ran on to the field. The men quickly ran past left fielder Jose Cardenal and stopped in left-center field. One of the men stooped to his knees, unscrewed the cap to a can of lighter fluid, and soaked the American flag with it. We all watched dumbstruck as the man pulled out a match and tried to light the American flag on fire.

"To the astonishment of the protestors, the fans, and those of us on the field, All-Star outfielder Rick Monday ran at the protestors, grabbed the burning flag, and ran towards the dugout as I screamed at the protestors from the third-base coaching box.

"The fans immediately got on their feet to recognize Monday's heroic act. And without any prompting that I can remember, the whole crowd stood and began to fill the stadium with an impromptu rendition of 'God Bless America.'

"News outlets around the country included the highlight that night on the evening news. Twenty years later, *The Sporting News* commemorated the event. Today, the flag burning incident is still shown in highlights. And everyone who saw the incident then, and now, knows that the protestors were doing something terrible, offensive, and wrong.

People on the other side of this issue will try to tell you that flag desecration or events like the ones I just described don't happen often enough, aren't offensive enough, or that they just aren't a big deal. They don't believe that 20 acts of flag desecration in the last 18 months is very many. But these people are wrong, just like the protestors that day in Dodger Stadium were.

"It is not how often a flag is desecrated that makes it wrong. Just because cross burnings don't happen every day doesn't mean that they are no longer wrong. If your son or daughter is caught breaking the law, do you tell them that what they did was not wrong because they'd never done it before?

"In poll after poll, more than 80 percent of Americans say that they want this amendment. Several statewide polls show similar results. In addition, legislatures in 49 states have passed resolutions urging Congress to pass the flag protection amendment.

"By joining the House in passing the amendment, the Senate can protect an honored symbol that ties every American together, while preserving our First Amendment rights. You can also send a very important message to the young people of this country: that respect for God and country are basic to what our nation stands for and are ideals worth honoring and protecting.

"I urge you to help teach our children about these ideals by passing this amendment and sending it to the states for ratification."

Vernon J. Biever

VINCE LOMBARDI

H e may have been the greatest motivator in the history of professional sports, this tough, granite-like Italian man from Brooklyn, New York, whose coaching method of precision and tough love with the championship Green Bay Packer teams made him an American legend.

Vincent Thomas Lombardi was born on June 11, 1913 in Brooklyn, New York. He had studied to be a priest, but his church was destined to be a football field, and he was a standout fullback for St. Francis Prep High School. Lombardi stayed in New York for college, and first gained acclaim as a player at Fordham University, where, as a lineman, he was known as one of the "Seven Blocks of Granite."

Lombardi graduated magna cum laude with a business major in 1937 from Fordham, and spent the next several years working at a finance company, going to law school at Fordham at night, and playing semi-pro football for the

Wilmington Clippers in Delaware. He began his coaching career in 1938 at St. Cecilia High School in Englewood, N.J., coaching football, basketball, and baseball. He stayed until 1947, when he went back to Fordham as an assistant coach.

Lombardi attracted the attention of one of the greatest coaches in the country, Earl "Colonel Red" Blaik, football coach for the United States Military Academy at West Point, who hired Lombardi as a defensive line coach in 1949. He stayed at West Point until 1954, when a former classmate, Jim Lee Howell, became the head coach of the New York Giants and called on Lombardi to join his staff as an assistant. Lombardi was in charge of the offense, while another future NFL head coach, Tom Landry, led the defense.

After helping mold the Giants into a championship squad, Lombardi finally got a chance to run the whole show on his own in the town of Green Bay, Wis., where he was named general manager and head coach of the Packers, who had won just one game in the season before Lombardi arrived. Using his hard-nosed style and a disciplined offensive attack that relied on the running game known as the Green Bay sweep, Lombardi turned the losing franchise into the gold standard for winning within three years, when, in 1961, the Packers pummeled his old team, the Giants, 37-0 to win the NFL championship.

Lombardi's winning ways continued. The Packers, under his tenure, won six division titles, five NFL championships and the first two Super Bowls against AFL teams. He had a record of 98-30-4 before retiring after the 1968 season to work exclusively in the Packers front office. However, Lombardi missed coaching too much to stay away from the sideline, and took an offer from Washington attorney Edward Bennett Williams to run the hapless Washington

Redskins in 1969. Lombardi turned a perennial loser into a winning team, posting a 7-5-1 record, the Redskins first winning season in 14 years.

Then tragedy struck. Lombardi died from stomach cancer on September 3, 1970. He was inducted into the Pro Football Hall of Fame in 1971 and the Super Bowl trophy was renamed the Vince Lombardi Super Bowl Trophy. And though an era ended when Lombardi passed away, his legacy lives on through his words that still ring true today.

VINCE LOMBARDI ON:

CHARACTER

"It is essential to understand that battles are primarily won in the hearts of men."

"Mental toughness is many things and rather difficult to explain. Its qualities are sacrifice and self-denial. Also, most importantly, it is combined with a perfectly disciplined will that refuses to give in. It's a state of mind—you could call it character in action."

COACHING

"They call it coaching but it is teaching. You do not just tell them, you show them the reasons."

"In spite of what you've heard, I can't walk on water, even when the Potomac is frozen."

—*After being hired to coach the Washington Redskins*

"Offensively, you do what you do best and you do it again and again. Defensively, you attack your opponent's strength."

COMMITMENT

"The quality of a person's life is in direct proportion to their commitment to excellence, regardless of their chosen field of endeavor."

"Once a man has made a commitment to a way of life, he puts the greatest strength in the world behind him. It's something we call heart power. Once a man has made this commitment, nothing will stop him short of success."

"Unless a man believes in himself and makes a total commitment to his career and puts everything he has into it—his mind, his body, and his heart—what is life worth to him? If I were a salesman, I would make this commitment to my company, to the product, and most of all, to myself."

CONFIDENCE

"Confidence is contagious and so is lack of confidence, and a customer will recognize both."

"I hold it more important to hold the players confidence than their affection."

DESIRE

"Once you learn to quit, it becomes a habit."

"If you aren't fired with enthusiasm, you'll be fired with enthusiasm."

DETERMINATION

"The difference between a successful person and others is not a lack of strength, not a lack of knowledge, but rather in a lack of will."

"The spirit, the will to win and the will to excel...these are the things that endure and these are the qualities that are so much more important than any of the events that occasion them."

"A man can be as great as he wants to be. If you believe in yourself and have the courage, the determination, the dedication, the competitive drive, and if you are willing to sacrifice the little things in life and pay the price for the things that are worthwhile, it can be done."

"If you'll not settle for anything less than your best, you will be amazed at what you can accomplish in your lives."

DISCIPLINE

"I've never known a man worth his salt who, in the long run, deep down in his heart, didn't appreciate the grind, the discipline. There is something good in men that really yearns for discipline."

"The good Lord gave you a body that can stand most anything. It's your mind you have to convince."

EDUCATION

"A school without football is in danger of deteriorating into a medieval study hall."

FAILURE

"In great attempts, it is glorious even to fail."

FOOTBALL

"Dancing is a contact sport. Football is a hitting sport."

"Football is like life: It requires perseverance, self-denial, hard work, sacrifice, dedication, and respect for authority."

"This is a game for madmen."

INJURIES

"If you can walk, you can run."

INTENSITY

"Mental toughness is essential to success."

"There's only one way to succeed in anything, and that is to give it everything. I do, and I demand that my players do."

LEADERSHIP

"Leadership rests not only upon ability, not only upon capacity; having the capacity to lead is not enough. The leader must be willing to use it. His leadership is then based on truth and character. There must be truth in the purpose and willpower in the character."

"Leadership is based on a spiritual quality; the power to inspire, the power to inspire others to follow."

"A leader must identify himself with the group, must back up the group, even at the risk of displeasing superiors. He must believe that the group wants from him a sense of approval. If this feeling prevails, production, discipline, morale will be high, and in return, you can demand the cooperation to promote the goals of the company."

"Leaders are made, they are not born. They are made by hard effort, which is the price which all of us must pay to achieve any goal that is worthwhile."

"It is essential to understand that battles are primarily won in the hearts of men. Men respond to leadership in a most remarkable way and once you have won his heart, he will follow you anywhere."

LOVE

"They may not love you at the time, but they will later."

MOTIVATION

"Coaches who can outline plays on a blackboard are a dime a dozen. The ones who win get inside their players and motivate them."

PERSEVERANCE

"It's not whether you get knocked down, it's whether you get up."

PREPARATION

"The harder you work, the harder it is to surrender."

"To me, the big thing in being a successful team is repetition of what you're doing, either by word of mouth, blackboard, or specifically by work on the field. You repeat, repeat, repeat as a unit."

SACRIFICE

"Football is a great deal like life in that it teaches that work, sacrifice, perseverance, competitive drive, selflessness, and respect for authority is the price each and every one of us must pay to achieve any goal that is worthwhile."

"Once you agree upon the price you and your family must pay for success, it enables you to ignore the minor hurts, the opponent's pressure, and the temporary failures."

SUCCESS

"Success demands singleness of purpose."

"To achieve success, whatever the job we have, we must pay a price."

"Success is like anything worthwhile. It has a price. You have to pay the price to win and you have to pay the price to get to the point where success is possible. Most important, you must pay the price to stay there."

"There's only one way to succeed in anything, and that is to give it everything. I do, and I demand that my players do."

TEAMWORK

"Individual commitment to a group effort: that is what makes a team work, a company work, a society work, a civilization work."

"Teams do not go physically flat, they go mentally stale."

"Teamwork is what the Green Bay Packers were all about.

They didn't do it for individual glory. They did it because they loved one another."

"People who work together will win, whether it be against complex football defenses, or the problems of modern society."

"The achievements of an organization are the results of the combined effort of each individual."

WINNING

"You never win a game unless you beat the guy in front of you. The score on the board doesn't mean a thing. That's for the fans. You've got to win the war with the man in front of you. You've got to get your man."

"Some of us will do our jobs well and some will not, but we will be judged by only one thing: the result."

"Winning is not a sometime thing, it's an all the time thing. You don't win once in a while; you don't do the right thing once in a while; you do them right all the time. Winning is a habit. Unfortunately, so is losing."

"Winning is not everything, but making effort to win is."

"It's easy to have faith in yourself and have discipline when you're a winner, when you're number one. What you've got to have is faith and discipline when you're not yet a winner."

WORK ETHIC

"The harder you work, the harder it is to surrender."

•••

Vince Lombardi, while he was coaching the Packers, once wrote about his philosophy of winning in an essay called "The Habit of Winning":

"Winning is not a sometime thing. You don't win once in a while. You don't do things right once in a while. You do them right all the time.

"Winning is a habit. Unfortunately, so is losing. There is no room for second place. There is only one place in my game, and that is first place. I have finished second twice in my time at Green Bay and I don't ever want to finish second again. There is a second place bowl game, but it is a game for losers played by losers. It is, and always has been, an American zeal to be first in anything we do, and to win, and to win, and to win.

"Every time a football player goes out to play, he's got to play from the ground up, from the soles of his feet right up to his head. Every inch of him has to play. Some guys play with their heads. That's okay—you've got to be smart to be number one in any business, but more important, you've got to play with your heart. With every fiber of your body. If you are lucky enough to find a guy with a lot of head and a lot of heart, he's never going to come off the field second.

"Running a football team is no different than running any other kind of organization—an army, a political party, or a business. The problems are the same. The objective is to win, to beat the other guy. Maybe that sounds hard or cruel. I don't think it is.

"It is a reality of life that men are competitive and the most competitive games draw the most competitive men. That's why they're here: to compete. They know the rules and the objectives when they get in the game. The objective is to win—fairly, squarely, decently, and by the rules—but to win. And in truth, I have never known a man worth his salt who, in the long run, deep down in his heart, did not appreciate the grind, the discipline. There is something in good men that really yearns for and needs discipline and the harsh reality of head-to-head combat.

"I don't say these things because I believe in the 'brute' nature of man, or that man must be brutalized to be combative. I believe in God and I believe in human decency. But I firmly believe that any man's finest hour, his greatest fulfillment to all he holds dear, is the moment when he has worked his heart out in a good cause and lies exhausted on the field of battle, victorious."

What others have said about Vince Lombardi:

"When Lombardi said 'sit down' we didn't look for a chair."

—Green Bay Packer tackle Forrest Gregg

"He made you a believer. He told you what the other team was going to do, and he told you what you had to do to beat them, and invariably he was right."

—Green Bay Packer defensive end Willie Davis

"He made us all better than we thought we could be."

—Green Bay Packer guard Jerry Kramer

"All he wanted from you was perfection."

—Green Bay Packer fullback Jim Taylor

"You might reduce Lombardi's coaching philosophy to a single sentence: In any game, you do the things you do best and you do them over and over and over."

—Chicago Bears owner and head coach George Halas

Managing

"I'd rather ride the buses managing in Triple A than be a lawyer."

—Baseball manager Tony LaRussa,
who is also an attorney

"There are three secrets to managing. The first secret is have patience. The second is be patient. And the third most important secret is patience."

—Baseball manager Chuck Tanner

"A manager's job is simple. For 162 games you try not to screw up all that smart stuff your organization did last December."

—Baseball manager Earl Weaver

"A manager has his cards dealt to him and he must play them."

—New York Yankees manager Miller Huggins

"Go with the best you've got."

—Baseball manager Al Lopez

"I'm not the manager because I'm always right, but I'm always right because I'm the manager."

—Baseball manager Gene Mauch

"I never got many questions about my managing. I tried to get 25 guys who didn't ask questions."

—Baseball manager Earl Weaver

"I don't think a manager should be judged by whether he wins the pennant, but by whether he gets the most out of the 25 men he's been given."

—Baseball manager Chuck Tanner

"The manager is by himself. He can't mingle with his players. I enjoyed my players, but I could not socialize with them, so I spent a lot of time alone in my hotel room. Those four walls kind of close in on you."

—Los Angeles Dodgers manager Walt Alston

"A manager doesn't hear the cheers."

—Baseball manager Alvin Dark

"Managing can be more discouraging than playing, especially when you're losing because when you're a player, there are at least individual goals you can shoot for. When you're a manager all the worries of the team become your worries."

—Baseball manager Al Lopez

"A manager should stay as far away as possible from his players. I don't know if I said 10 words to Frank Robinson while he played for me."

—Baseball manager Earl Weaver

"I'm happy for him [Gil Hodges]. That is, if you think becoming a big league manager is a good thing to have happen to you."

—Los Angeles Dodgers manager Walt Alston when asked to comment about one of his former players, Gil Hodges, becoming a major league manager

"When I get through managing, I'm going to open up a kindergarten."

—Baseball manager Billy Martin

"The toughest thing about managing is standing up for nine innings."

—Baseball manager Paul Owens

"Bad ballplayers make good managers, not the other way around. All I can do is help them be as good as they are."

—Baseball manager Earl Weaver

MARRIAGE

"Divorce, no. Murder, yes."

—Anne Hayes, on whether she ever considered leaving her husband, Ohio State football coach Woody Hayes

"When I asked, 'How would you like to be married to a major league manager?' my wife said, 'What, is Tommy Lasorda getting a divorce?'"

—John Wathan after being hired as manager of the Kansas City Royals

"When I got home after practice one night, my wife met me at the door crying. 'Darling, the dog ate the meat loaf I made for you.' I took her in my arms and said, 'Stop crying, honey. I'll buy you another dog.'"

—Basketball coach Abe Lemons

"I really don't know. I don't see her that much."

—Football coach Ray Perkins when asked about how his wife feels about his long working hours

MISTAKES

"What to do with a mistake: Recognize it, admit it, learn from it, forget it."

—North Carolina basketball coach Dean Smith

"He makes too many senseless errors. He has this little gong that goes off, saying, 'Hey, this time I'll do something different.' That's when I swallow my tobacco."

—San Francisco Giants manager Charlie Fox on second baseman Tito Fuentes

"You don't win by making sensational plays; you win by not making mistakes."

—Football coach Bum Phillips

"The hero of a thousand plays becomes a bum after one error."

—Football coach Bob Zuppke

"I'm wrong often, very often, and say it all the time."

—Football coach Steve Spurrier

MONEY

"You can have money piled to the ceiling, but the size of your funeral is still going to depend on the weather."

—Baseball manager Chuck Tanner

"I'm independently wealthy. I have enough money to live for the rest of my life—providing I die tomorrow."

—Basketball coach Bill Fitch

"When you're playing for money, winning is the only thing that matters."

—Baseball manager Leo Durocher

"Players' salaries have been on the space shuttle and coaches salaries have been on the escalator."

—Hockey coach Terry Murray

MORALE

"The most important thing is team morale."

—North Carolina basketball coach Dean Smith

MOTIVATION

"Never leave a field with a boy feeling you're mad at him. You can chew him out, but then pat him on the shoulder."

—Florida A&M football coach Jake Gaither

"You can motivate players better with kind words than you can with a whip."

—Oklahoma football coach Bud Wilkinson

"The ones who want to achieve and win championships motivate themselves."

—Football coach and television analyst Mike Ditka

"You can lead a horse to water, but you can't stick his head in it."

—Baseball manager Paul Owens

OFFENSE

"Some nights it's going to be like hunting bear with a butter knife."

*—Boston Bruins hockey coach Pat Burns
on his team's poor offensive play*

OLYMPICS

"It's national pride, it's legacy, it's history. The Olympics transcend the game itself."

—Hockey coach Herb Brooks

OPENING DAY

"The outfield was snow-covered. Ground balls made a line as they went through. There were about 12 streakers. You really had to want to be a streaker that day."

*—New York Mets manager Bobby Valentine
referring to a 1974 opening day in Chicago*

181

OPPORTUNITY

"Never surrender opportunity for security."

—*Baseball manager and general manager Branch Rickey*

OWNERS

"You have to bear in mind that Mr. Autry's favorite horse was named Champion. He ain't ever had one called Runner Up."

—*California Angels manager Gene Mauch talking about his team's owner, former Cowboy film star Gene Autry*

Passion

"Do what you love to do and give it your very best. Whether it's business or baseball, or the theater, or any field. If you don't love what you're doing and you can't give it your best, get out of it. Life is too short. You'll be an old man before you know it."

—*Baseball manager Al Lopez*

"The youngsters coming up now just go through the motions necessary to make the play. They should bounce around a little, show some life and zip. It adds a little action and gives the fans something to look at rather than the monotonous routine, no matter how perfectly the play is made."

—*Los Angeles Dodgers manager Walt Alston*

People

"People are needed, but nobody is necessary."

—*NFL coach and owner Paul Brown*

PERFORMANCE

"The films look suspiciously like the game itself."

—*Houston Oilers football coach Bum Phillips when asked*
if the game films revealed anything after a loss

"I suppose you know why I took you out. You see the American League record for striking out is five times in one game and I didn't want you [Jimmie Dykes] to tie it in your very first game."

—*Philadelphia Athletics owner and manager*
Connie Mack explaining to Jimmie Dykes why
he took him out of the game

"What you do should speak so loudly that no one can hear what you say."

—*Football coach Marv Levy*

PERSISTENCE

"Paralyze resistance with persistence."

—*Ohio State football coach Woody Hayes*

PERSPECTIVE

"You're never as good as everyone tells you when you win, and you're never as bad as they say when you lose."

—*Football coach Lou Holtz*

"If it doesn't bother you, it won't bother them."

—*Tennessee women's basketball coach Pat Summitt*

"If you make every game a life-or-death proposition, you're going to have problems. For one thing, you'll be dead a lot."

—*North Carolina basketball coach Dean Smith*

"I'm just a caraway seed in the bakery of life."

—*Basketball coach Pete Gillen*

"Where else would you rather be, than right here, right now?"

—*Football coach Marv Levy's comments to players before a game*

"Don't sweat the small stuff."

—*Football coach Kevin Gilbride*

PHYSIQUE

"The boy's [Hack Wilson] got talent and desire, but he ain't got no neck."

—*New York Giants manager John McGraw on the unusual physical characteristics of slugger Hack Wilson*

PITCHING

"The most important things in life are good friends and a strong bullpen."

—*Baseball manager Bob Lemon*

"If you don't have outstanding relief pitching, you might as well piss on the fire and call in the dogs."

—Baseball manager Whitey Herzog

"You just listen to the ball and bat come together. They make an awful noise."

—Baseball manager Darrell Johnson
on when to change pitchers

"Nobody likes to hear it, because it's dull, but the reason you win or lose is darn near always the same: pitching."

—Baseball manager Earl Weaver

PLAYERS

"I never criticize a player unless they are convinced of my unconditional confidence in them."

—NFL and college football coach John Robinson

"The country is full of good coaches. What it takes to win is a bunch of interested players."

—Football coach Don Coryell

"Treat each player as your own son/daughter if you can...the parents have invested in you."

—College basketball coach Hank Iba

"Two kinds of ball players aren't worth a darn: One that never does what he's told, and one who does nothin' except what he's told."

—Football coach Bum Phillips

"Players' attention spans get less and less as they progress."

—*Duke basketball coach Mike Krzyzewski*

"I know, Jim, but the outfielders are."

—*Baseball manager Jeff Torborg, taking pitcher Jim Kern out of the game. Kern responded that he wasn't tired*

POLITICS

"You know, this guy fired me. The honest truth is that I would campaign barefoot for him today."

—*New York Mets manager Bobby Valentine on Republican presidential candidate George W. Bush, who was Valentine's boss, previously, as an owner of the Texas Rangers and had fired Valentine as the team's manager*

"Any pitcher who throws at a batter and deliberately tries to hit him is a communist."

—*Baseball manager Alvin Dark*

POPULARITY

"I'm not trying to win a popularity poll. I'm trying to win football games. I don't like nice people. I like tough, honest people."

—*Football coach Woody Hayes*

POTENTIAL

"I can't believe that God put us on this earth to be ordinary."

—*Football coach Lou Holtz*

"Potential is synonymous with getting your ass kicked."

—*Hockey coach Kevin Constantine*

"Don't rate potential over performance."

—*Football coach Jim Fassel*

PRACTICE

"It was about normal, no worse than an ordinary death march."

—*Football coach Lou Holtz on spring practice*

"There'll be two buses leaving the hotel for the park tomorrow. The 2 o'clock bus will be for those of you who need a little extra work. The empty bus will be leaving at 5 o'clock."

—*Dave Bristol, manager of the San Francisco Giants, telling his players they need work*

"The one place at Michigan State I was never late to was practice. It didn't start until I got there."

—*Michigan State football coach Duffy Daugherty*

"You better have great practices."

—*Basketball coach Al McGuire*

PRAISE

"Praise your kids. Inspire and motivate your players with praise. Ten years from now it won't matter what your record was. Will your kids love you or hate you?"

—*Basketball coach Jim Harrick*

"Only praise behavior that you want to be repeated. Never use false praise."

—North Carolina basketball coach Dean Smith

"There's nothing greater in the world than when somebody on the team does something good, and everybody gathers around to pat him on the back."

—Baseball manager Billy Martin

PREPARATION

"Winning is the science of being totally prepared."

—NFL coach George Allen

"You play the way you practice. Practice the right way, and you will play the right way."

—Football coach Pop Warner

"The thrill isn't in the winning, it's in the doing."

—Football coach Chuck Noll

"The will to prepare is the key ingredient to success."

—Oklahoma football coach Bud Wilkinson

"We put a premium on knowing what the other team does. Then we try to take them out of it."

—Basketball coach P.J. Carlesimo

"Coaching is preparation."

—Princeton basketball coach Pete Carril

"If you want to catch more fish, use more hooks."

—Football coach George Allen

"Prepare for every game like you just lost your last game."

—Basketball coach Lon Kruger

"Everyone wants to win. The special person has the will to prepare to win."

—Football coach Marv Levy

PRESSURE

"Pressure is something you feel when you don't know what you're doing."

—Pittsburgh Steelers football coach Chuck Noll

PRIDE

"I don't care if I was a ditch-digger at a dollar a day, I'd want to do my job better than the fellow next to me. I'd want to be the best at whatever I do."

—Baseball manager and general manager Branch Rickey

PROBLEMS

"Problems are the price you pay for progress."

—Baseball manager and general manager Branch Rickey

College Football Hall of Fame
South Bend, Ind.

Joe Paterno has always represented more than just excellence in coaching college football; and he is that, with the greatest record of any college coach in history, with more than 330 wins, two national championships, and undefeated teams in 1968, 1969, 1973, and 1994.

Paterno has been seen as a symbol of what is good and right about college athletics, and his voice has always been one that stood for honesty and hard work in the more than 50 years he has been part of Penn State football. Because of that status, when Joe Paterno talks, his words carry tremendous weight.

Born in Brooklyn, New York, on December 21, 1926, Paterno went to St. Edmond's Grammar School and Brooklyn Prep. He went in the service during World War II, and then accepted an athletic scholarship to Brown University when he got out of the Army. He was an English major at Brown and also their star quarterback, playing under coach Rip Engle. Paterno also played two years of basketball at

Brown, and his coach was the future Pro Football Hall of Fame coach Weeb Ewbank.

Paterno graduated in 1950 and his career at Penn State began right after that when he was hired as an assistant coach under Engle, who took the job at Penn State. In 1966, Paterno took over the head coaching job and began to compile a legacy never seen before in college football.

He needed fewer games (246) to reach the 200-win plateau than any major college coach, and was also the quickest to achieve 300 victories. He has had 26 teams finish in the Top 20. Penn State has won the Lambert-Meadowlands Trophy for Eastern football supremacy 21 times in Paterno's coaching run.

His bowl record is remarkable, leading all college coaches with 30 bowl appearances. He has taken Nittany Lion teams to the Fiesta Bowl six times, the Orange Bowl four times, the Sugar Bowl four times, the Citrus Bowl three times, the Cotton Bowl twice, the Gator Bowl twice, the Blockbuster Bowl twice, the Outback Bowl twice, and also trips to the Liberty Bowl, Aloha Bowl, Rose Bowl, and Alamo Bowl.

Paterno has been named Coach of the Year an unprecedented four times in voting conducted by the American Football Coaches Association. More than 200 of his players have gone on to careers in the NFL, and has had players win all of the major college awards: the Heisman, Maxwell, Lombardi, O'Brien, Outland, and Biletnikoff awards.

Just as important to Paterno's legacy, though, and symbolic of what he has stood for during his career, he has coached 20 first-team Academic All-Americans, 14 Hall of Fame Scholar-Athletes, and 16 NCAA postgraduate scholarship winners. In December 1991, Paterno became the first active coach to receive the National Football Foundation and College Football Hall of Fame "Distinguished American" award. He was the first football coach named by *Sports Illustrated* as its "Sportsman of the Year."

He and his wife, Sue, have given Penn State $3.5 million to endow faculty positions and scholarships, and to support two building projects. This is believed to be the most generous gift ever made by a collegiate coach and his family to a university. He has been part of numerous fund-raising drives for educational facilities at the school, and has turned down several offers to coach in the NFL.

Paterno has become such a popular icon that efforts have been made numerous times in Pennsylvania to convince him to run for office. But he has remained devoted to education and football and has been the standard-bearer for honor in college sports.

JOE PATERNO ON:

COACHING

"What are coaches? Number one, we're teachers and we're educators. We have the same obligations as all teachers at our institutions, except we probably have more influence over our young people than anyone other than their families.

"We're dealing with emotions; we're dealing with commitment; we're dealing with discipline, and loyalty, and pride. The things that make a difference in a person's life—pride, loyalty, and commitment—are the things that make a difference in this country. We're teaching them [student-athletes] the realities of the competitive life."

"I think anybody who goes into college coaching these days is nuts. It is just so demanding. People expect you to be Moses."

CONFIDENCE

"The minute you think you've got it made, disaster is just around the corner."

"Act like you expect to get into the end zone."

"You need to play with supreme confidence, or else you'll lose again, and then losing becomes a habit."

"Besides pride, loyalty, discipline, heart, and mind, confidence is the key to all the locks."

"Believe deep down in your heart that you're destined to do great things."

EDUCATION

"The purpose of college football is to serve education, not the other way around. I hound my players to get involved. Ten years from now I want them to look back on college as a wonderful time of expanding themselves—not just four years of playing football."

"The players who have been most important to the success of Penn State teams have just naturally kept their priorities straight: football a high second, but academics an undisputed first."

"I really don't want a kid to leave here saying, 'If they had gotten on my back a little more, I might have gotten a more meaningful education.' I have been very fortunate that I had a great education. I appreciate it. People talk about my longevity. If I were honest with people, I feel that my education really made it possible for me to handle some situations that some other people haven't handled."

EXPLOITATION

"We have raped a generation of young black athletes. We have taken kids and sold them on a bouncing ball and running with a football and that being able to do certain things athletically was an end in itself. We cannot afford to do that to another generation."

FOOTBALL

"Football is a great game. It demands a young man's total commitment—emotionally, mentally, and physically. It challenges our young people to do their very best, to discipline themselves to develop mental, as well as physical, toughness. At its best, it is a wonderful and worthwhile experience, which will have immense future character benefits for its players."

"Football can be an intellectual exercise and I want people who will think about what we can do and not be content to rubber-stamp my thoughts or be satisfied with what has worked in the past."

GEOGRAPHY

"I'm not worried about me. If I wake up some morning and say someone else can do a better job, I'll tell Sue, 'Let's go to Italy or maybe back to Brooklyn.' Either one of those two countries is good enough for me."

GHOSTS

"Knute Rockne won't be out there to put a spell on you. The Four Horsemen aren't going to be around. Nobody's going to put a curse on you. I don't believe in ghosts, so you shouldn't believe in ghosts. The best 11 will win."

GREATNESS

"Don't just stand back and play the way you're coached. A great player must rise to the occasion and turn the game around on his own."

LEADERS

"We need people who influence their peers and can't be detoured from their convictions by their peers that don't have any convictions."

LOSING

"Losing a game is heartbreaking. Losing your sense of excellence or worth is a tragedy."

"I just hate to lose. I know I preach a lot about being willing to lose, that there can be valor in losing to a better opponent, but I have never learned how not to hate losing."

"Did you ever get the crap kicked out of you? Well, you just saw Penn State get the crap kicked out of it."

—*After Nebraska defeated Penn State 44-6 in the 1993 Kickoff Classic*

MORALE

"You don't have to concern yourself with how a first stringer feels. The real test is whether the last substitute has good morale. If he has, it means everybody has."

NOISE

"Loudness is great if you're playing well."

PENN STATE

"After a few weeks I told Rip, 'I'm getting out of here before I go nuts in this town. You better start looking for another coach.'"

—His reaction after first coming to State College, Pa.

"Penn State has been very good to both Sue and me. We've met some wonderful people here. We've known many students who have gone on to become outstanding leaders in their professions and in society, and all of our children have received a first-class education here. I've never felt better about Penn State and its future potential than I do right now."

—After he and his wife donated
$3.5 million to the school

PERFORMANCE

"You have to perform at a consistently higher level than others. That's the mark of a true professional."

POLITICS

"I'd like to know how could the president know so little about Watergate in 1973 and so much about college football in 1969."

—Speaking about President Richard M. Nixon,
who resigned office in 1974, and how Nixon had
declared Texas national champions in 1969
over an undefeated Penn State team

PREPARATION

"The will to win is important, but the will to prepare is vital."

"I've got a checklist for everything. I've got a checklist for a checklist."

PUBLICITY

"Publicity is like poison; it doesn't hurt unless you swallow it."

SPORTSWRITERS

"If I ever need a brain transplant, I want one from a sports-writer, because I'll know it's never been used."

SUCCESS

"Success is never final. Failure is never fatal."

"Success without honor is an unseasoned dish; it will satisfy your hunger, but it won't taste good."

TEAMS

"When a team outgrows individual performance and learns team confidence, excellence becomes a reality."

UNIFORMS

"I don't think our uniforms look that bad. I think they say something to kids about team-oriented play and an austere approach to life."

VALUES

"I think my top priority in life is to be a good husband and a good father. Then I hope to be a good influence on the young people with whom I come in contact to be a decent role model for them. I'd like to help them understand that values are important."

WINNING

"Just winning is a silly reason to be serious about a game. For a kid still in school, devotion to winning football games at nearly any cost may cripple his mind for life. Institutions of higher learning don't have the moral right to exploit and mislead inexperienced kids that way."

"What counts in sports is not the victory, but the magnificence of the struggle."

"Winning is a matter of knowing how to win."

"For committing yourself to winning the game, whether you win it or not, you always pay in tears and blood."

WORK

"Our players work so hard in practice, Saturdays seem easy by comparison."

WHAT OTHERS HAVE SAID ABOUT JOE PATERNO:

"He's tough as hell, but he does things the way they're supposed to be done. He follows the rules. He believes you're there for an education. He teaches you more than football. He teaches you about life."

—*Former Penn State linebacker Shane Conlon*

"He doesn't understand how much he helped us, not just from a football standpoint, but from an emotional and dedication standpoint, He doesn't realize how much so many guys out there think of him. And if you walked in a room, walked up to him and said, 'Thank you,' he wouldn't want to hear it. He wouldn't even want to listen to it. But he needs to hear it. He needs to have people come back and say thanks. It's no different than it is with your own father. He was my father when I was here."

—*Former Penn State receiver Kenny Jackson*

RACE

"Jackie [Robinson], we've got no army. There's virtually nobody on our side. No owners, no umpires, very few newspapermen. And I'm afraid that many fans will be hostile. We'll be in a tough position. We can win only if we can convince the world that I'm doing this because you're a great ballplayer, a fine gentleman."

—Baseball manager and general manager Branch Rickey, speaking to Jackie Robinson about the challenge of breaking the color line in Major League Baseball

"The only thing in this country that blacks really dominate, except for poverty, is basketball."

—Basketball coach Al McGuire

"I don't care if the guy [Jackie Robinson] is yellow or black, or if he has stripes like a zebra. I'm the manager of this team and I say he plays."

—Baseball manager Leo Durocher when asked about Robinson breaking the color line and playing on his 1947 Brooklyn Dodger squad

"Ethnic prejudice has no place in sports, and baseball must recognize that truth if it is to maintain stature as a national game."

—Baseball manager and general manager Branch Rickey

REFEREES

"I know why we lost the Civil War. We must have had the same officials."

—Coach Bum Phillips on losing the Senior Bowl

"You can say something to popes, kings, and presidents, but you can't talk to officials. In the next war, they should give everybody a whistle."

—Basketball coach Abe Lemons

"You have to be respectful when arguing with an official. I usually say, 'Sir, are we watching the same game?'"

—Football coach Homer Smith

Maybe aliens came down and took over his helmet."

—Carolina hockey coach Paul Maurice
on late penalty calls by a referee

REJECTION

"Expect rejection but expect more to overcome it."

—Football coach Marv Levy

RESPECT

"Your players' attitude toward you hinges on just one thing, and that is respect. If they do not respect you, you've lost them. If you have their respect, you've got it made."

—Oklahoma football coach Bud Wilkinson

RESPONSIBILITY

"The most important quality I look for in a player is accountability. You've got to be accountable for who you are. It's too easy to blame things on someone else."

—Basketball coach Lenny Wilkins

"The trouble with athletes today is that they are great at rationalizing. Too many won't stand up and take the blame and admit they didn't produce. When one does, you have a rare man."

—Basketball coach and television analyst Hubie Brown

RETIREMENT

"I think it's wise to back off before you leave feet first or somebody tells you it's time to go."

—Nebraska football coach Tom Osborne

"I ain't doing a damn thing, and I don't start until noon."

—Football coach Bum Phillips on his retirement schedule

REVENGE

"If they throw one at your head, you throw twice. If they throw twice, you throw four times."

—Baseball manager Leo Durocher instructing his pitchers on when to hit batters

RIVALRIES

"When it's said and done, it will just be three games on the schedule and it won't mean a hoot."

—New York Mets manager Bobby Valentine on the inaugural regular season series between the Mets and the New York Yankees

"I think there should be bad blood between all clubs."

—Baseball manager Earl Weaver

RULES

"The fewer rules a coach has, the fewer rules there are for players to break."

—Football coach and broadcaster John Madden

"I believe in rules. Sure I do. If there weren't any rules, how could you break them?"

—Baseball manager Leo Durocher

College Football Hall of Fame
South Bend, Ind.

EDDIE ROBINSON

Eddie Robinson is the best example of a historic figure you will find when the story of college football in the 20th century is written. In 1966, the Football Writer's Association named him the "coach who made the biggest contribution to college football in the past 25 years." But he was far from finished. Eddie Robinson was the face and voice of Grambling University football from 1941 to 2000, and compiled an unparalleled record, a 408-178 mark.

Robinson was born on February 13, 1919, in Jackson, Louisiana, and it was in Louisiana where he would stay.

When Robinson was hired in 1941, Grambling was known as the Colored Industrial and Agricultural Institute of Lincoln Parish. The team went 3-5 in his first season, but he put his imprint on the school program in his second year, when the school had a 9-0 record. Not only were they unbeaten, but they were unscored upon as well. From 1943 to 1944, the school had no football team because of the war, so Robinson coached Grambling High School, and won a state championship.

He returned to coaching Grambling University and built up a program that would achieve perfection in 1955, posting a 10-0 record, the best in school history. In 1957, Robinson gained his 100th win, a 20-12 victory over Bethune-Cookman. In 1959, Grambling joined the Southwest Athletic Conference, and won the conference co-championship the following year. He won his 200th game in 1971, a 20-15 victory over Mississippi Valley State. In 1974 and 1975, Grambling won 16 straight games, the longest winning streak in school history. The 300th win was a 43-21 victory over Florida A&M in 1982, and three years later Robinson put himself at the top of coaching history when he got his 324th career win, passing Bear Bryant. In 1995, he hit 400 career wins with a 42-6 victory over Mississippi Valley State, and his final win also came against Mississippi Valley, a 20-13 victory in 1997.

When Eddie Robinson retired, he left behind a record of success that may never be matched. He sent several hundred players to the pro football ranks, including Paul "Tank" Younger, Buck Buchanan, Ernie Ladd, Willie Davis, James Harris, and Doug Williams. The new Grambling football stadium that opened in 1983 was named Robinson Stadium. He had a street named after him in Baton Rouge. He was the first Division I-AA coach and African-American to receive Bobby Dodd Coach of the Year Award.

Now there is an award called the Eddie Robinson Award, because what this man did—and said—is worth honoring.

EDDIE ROBINSON ON:

ACHIEVEMENT

"The will to win, the desire to succeed, the urge to reach your full potential. These are the keys that will unlock the door to personal excellence."

AMERICA

"If I ever doubted this was the greatest country in the world, I don't now."

—Retiring after 57 seasons as Grambling football coach

CHARACTER

"You have to go out and find the players, but they have to be good people. The football players are the most important people to me. I like being around them. I like teaching and seeing them succeed in life. That gives me the greatest thrill."

COACHING

"I enjoyed the coaching and would be lying if I said I didn't. But I wanted to be more than just a football coach."

"My parents would carry us to the high school games and they were always concerned why I wanted to be around the bench all of the time. I wanted to be around the bench to see what the coach was doing. It was then, around the third or fourth grade, that I realized I wanted to be a football coach, so I started reading everything I could about the game."

"Being coach. It's all I ever wanted to be."

"Coaching is the most rewarding profession in the world."

FAMILY

"The record I'm most proud of is that I've had only one job and one wife."

"We started courting around the end of elementary school, so she's always been there for me. She's an important part of my foundation."

—Speaking of his wife, Doris Robinson

FOOTBALL

"You play the game of football just the way you play the game of life."

HALL OF FAME

"The Hall of Fame, as the world knows, is the elite circle where many of the truly great contributors to the game of football are enshrined. I am thankful and very, very proud that you have chosen me on my merits and my career as a coach ranking with the truly immortals of this game."

—After being inducted into the
College Football Hall of Fame

Leadership

"Leadership, like coaching, is fighting for the hearts and souls of men and getting them to believe in you."

Life

"If I had the decision to make, I'd want to be born in America, go to work for Grambling, and marry the woman I married. I'd want to have the same children I had. I've had a good life."

Players

"Either get a better player or get a player better."

"My players can wear their hair as long as they want and dress any way they want. That is, if they can afford to pay their own tuition, meals, and board."

Winning

"I've never been concerned with personal records. All the 324 wins means is that I have been around for a long time."

—After passing Bear Bryant on the all-time college football winning list for coaches

Work ethic

"I've become a credit to my life on the farm [near Jackson, Louisiana]. It taught me the value of hard work, how to accept and overcome adversity, pride in a job well done. They are lessons I've never forgot and always use."

WHAT OTHERS HAVE SAID ABOUT EDDIE ROBINSON:

"He'd cry before a big game. He'd cry so hard that you'd be crying. Oh, would he cry."

—Former Grambling quarterback Doug Williams on Robinson's pre-game talks

"Nobody has ever done, or will ever do, what Eddie Robinson has done for this game. Our profession will never, ever be able to repay Eddie Robinson."

—Penn State football coach Joe Paterno talking about Robinson as one of his peers

"We owe so much of our life, our success in life, to him. He had an impact on social change as much as anyone, lifting the quality of education, the whole notion of black pride, individual consideration of equality, being able to compete given the opportunity. History won't fully record the significance of that impact."

—Willie Davis, a former player of Robinson's who went on to be a star defensive end for the Green Bay Packers

National Baseball Hall of Fame Library
Cooperstown, N.Y.

FRANK ROBINSON

F rank Robinson made his mark in baseball as one of the all-time best, and perhaps the most intense, players the game has ever seen, and his words often conveyed that intensity.

When he retired after the 1976 season, Robinson had compiled remarkable numbers over his playing career with the Cincinnati Reds, Baltimore Orioles, Los Angeles Dodgers, California Angels, and Cleveland Indians: 586 home runs, 1,812 runs batted in, and a .294 average over 2,808 games in his 20-year career. He was a Most Valuable Player in both leagues, with the Reds in the National League in 1961 and with the Orioles in the American League in 1966, and played on two World Series championship teams for the Orioles. One in 1966 against the Los Angeles Dodgers when he won the Triple Crown, leading the AL in home runs with 49, RBI with 122, and a .316 batting average. And the second in 1970 against the Cincinnati Reds. Robinson was also on three other pennant-winning teams: the Reds in 1961 and the Orioles in 1969 and 1971.

Besides his talent, what Robinson was also known for was the intense manner in which he approached the game—a hard, take-no-prisoners style, an overwhelming will to win. That was illustrated by his willingness to face tough pitchers and not back out of the box. He set a record as a rookie in 1956 by being hit with pitches 20 times.

But he became more than just a great ballplayer after the 1974 season ended. When the Cleveland Indians hired Frank Robinson, he joined another Robinson, Jackie, among the great social sports icons of the 20th century. Just as Jackie Robinson had broken the color barrier on the playing field in 1947, Frank Robinson broke it in the dugout by becoming the first black manager (initially a player-manager) in baseball.

On that historic opening day of 1975, Rachel Robinson, widow of Jackie, threw out the first ball in Cleveland, and Frank Robinson added to the drama by hitting a home run to lead the Indians to a 5-3 win over the New York Yankees. Robinson brought that same intensity that sustained him through his playing career, and led the Indians to their first winning record (81-78, fourth place) since 1968 and in 1976, their third .500-plus season since 1959, but he was fired when the Indians got off to a slow start in 1977. After coaching stints with the Angels and the Orioles, and managing the Orioles Class AAA club in Rochester, Robinson got another major league managing job in San Francisco managing the Giants in 1981. The Giants were competitive during his first two seasons, and finished just two games out of first place in the NL West in 1982—the same year Robinson was inducted into the National Baseball Hall of Fame—but was fired in August 1985.

In 1986 he went back to Baltimore as a coach, where he was a fan favorite, and within the first two weeks of the 1988 season, took over as manager of the Orioles after Cal

Ripken, Sr. was fired when the team lost its first six games of the season. Robinson would initially preside over the worst losing record in Major League Baseball history, as they went on to lose 21 straight games. But in 1989, with a club that did not appear to have much talent, Robinson led the Orioles to a second-place finish in the AL East, and they were not eliminated until the last series of the year against the division-leading Toronto Blue Jays.

In May 1991, Robinson was fired as the Orioles manager, but stayed with the team as an assistant general manager until he left after the 1995 season. Robinson was later hired by Major League Baseball in 2000 to be in charge of on-field disciplinary matters, but returned to the dugout for one more stint as manager of the Montreal Expos in 2002—a unique managing job in that the Expos are owned by Major League Baseball and marked for extinction by the end of the 2002 season. He was philosophical about his job with the Expos, but still was able to convey his feelings about the seemingly lost practice of intensity that he brought to the game.

Frank Robinson on:

Competing

"Close don't count in baseball. Close only counts in horseshoes and grenades."

Fans

"The fan is the one who suffers. He cheers a guy to a .350 season then watches that player sign with another team. When you destroy fan loyalties, you destroy everything."

—Referring to free agency in baseball and the movement of players from one team to another

FRATERNIZING

"There's absolutely no way you can go barreling into second and dump a guy on a double play, like you should do, when you've been fraternizing with him before a game."

HITTING

"Everybody's looking for a guy who can lead off. But whoever they put up there now doesn't do the things a leadoff hitter used to be called upon to do. Going deep in the count, bunting, stealing a base, that type of thing—getting on base any way you can—that doesn't seem to matter now. Each position used to be defined, from one to eight. These days, you put people in a lineup and say, 'Go get 'em.'"

—Referring to the demise of discipline in leadoff hitters

INTENSITY

"I don't see anyone playing in the major leagues today who combines both the talent and the intensity that I had. I always tried to do the best. I knew I couldn't always be the best, but I tried to be."

—Speaking in 1982 about the level of intensity of
ballplayers during that period

MANAGING

"If I had one wish in the world today, it would be that Jackie Robinson could be here to see this happen."

—Addressing a 1974 press conference after
Robinson became the first black manager
in the history of Major League Baseball

"I have heard of managers who encourage players not to slide hard for fear they will get hurt and be lost from the lineup for a time. That is why you occasionally see a player go into second base on a double-play ball and not even bother to slide. I wonder, could Ty Cobb sit through plays like that and hold his lunch?"

"It's nice to come into a town and be referred to as the manager of the Cleveland Indians instead of as the first black manager."

"No, I don't think my presence will cause an increase in black attendance at Cleveland. People come out to see the players. When do you see a manager anyway? When he's out on the field arguing with the umpires, making a fool of himself and you know you can't win, and when he brings out the line-up card."

—After being hired to manage the Cleveland Indians

"Managers don't have as much leverage as they used to have. We can't really be the boss. If I say to a veteran player, 'If you don't perform, you may be sent back to the minors,' they look at me and say, 'Who are you kidding? I'm not going anyplace. I've already had three years in the major leagues and you can't send me back to the minor leagues without my okay.'"

PENNANTS

"In Cleveland, pennant fever usually ends up being just a 48-hour virus."

PITCHERS

"Pitchers did me a favor when they knocked me down. It made me more determined. I wouldn't let that pitcher get me out. They say you can't hit if you're on your back, but I didn't hit on my back. I got up."

"Probably the most dramatic change in pitching I've observed in my years in baseball has been the disappearance of the knockdown or brushback pitch. This is why record numbers of home runs are flying out of ballparks, why earned run averages are soaring, and why there are so few 20 game winners in the majors."

PLAYERS

"The players today haven't been schooled coming up the ranks on what you're supposed to do. They don't take a pitch. They're allowed to swing, so they're down at the end of the bat, swinging from their rear ends."

—Talking about modern-day ballplayers after taking over the Montreal Expos job in 2002

"If the guys on the bench were as good as the guys you have out there, they'd be out there in first place."

"I had no trouble communicating, the players just didn't like what I had to say."

PRESENCE

"I hope they're not intimidated. I hope they feel like I'm approachable. I think I've made myself available to them where they would feel that they could come in and ask if they could go pick up their wife at the airport. I'd say sure, buddy, but don't drive fast. Drive slow."

—Responding to a question about how his players might approach him in his new job as manager of the Montreal Expos in 2002

PRESSURE

"You don't really know people until you get in the trenches with them, know how they think, know how they feel, know how they react."

RACISM

"If I don't speak up and speak out, who will? I think I owe that to Jackie and the other players to do whatever I can to help the cause."

ROBINSONS

"I don't see why you reporters keep confusing Brooks and me. Can't you see that we wear different numbers."

—Joking with reporters about the two Robinsons, Brooks (white) and Frank (black), on the Baltimore Orioles

STRATEGY

"You only have 27 outs and they're precious. I have no intention of giving away outs. But the bunt can be extremely important."

"The baselines belong to the runner, and whenever I was running the bases, I always slid hard. I wanted infielders to have that instant's hesitation about coming across the bag at second or about standing in there awaiting a throw to make a tag. There are only 27 outs in a ballgame, and it was my job to save one for my team every time I possibly could."

College Football Hall of Fame
South Bend, Ind.

KNUTE ROCKNE

nute Rockne was known as the father of college football and a master motivator, so legendary that it his words were immortalized by Hollywood in the infamous, "Win one for the Gipper" speech in the film, *Knute Rockne—All American*.

Rockne began his life's journey not in the U.S., but in Voss, Norway, where he was born on March 4, 1988. His family came to America shortly after that and settled in Chicago. Much to his parents' dismay, he fell in love with the American rough and tumble game of football, playing it in high school and on the sandlots of Chicago.

Rockne was determined to play football at Notre Dame, but had to work for four years in the Chicago Post Office to raise money for his education. He would eventually go to school at Notre Dame and play football, earning recognition as an All-American defensive end and captain of the team in his senior year. He was also an excellent student, and graduated magna cum laude in 1913. In fact, it was his academic standing that started his coaching career at Notre Dame. Rockne was offered a post at Notre Dame as a graduate assistant in chemistry—a job he took, provided he was allowed to help head football coach Jesse Harper. When Harper retired after the 1917 season, Rockne got the head coaching job, and began building the Notre Dame powerhouse program that became one of the standards of college football in the 20th century.

In the 13 years Rockne coached at Notre Dame, they won 105 games and lost just 12, with 5 ties. They had five undefeated and untied seasons. The coach produced 20 first-team All-Americans from his squads, and coached the legendary "Four Horsemen" that sportswriter Grantland Rice immortalized when the Irish faced Army in a 1924 game. Rice wrote, "Outlined against a blue, gray October sky the Four Horsemen rode again," referring to the backfield of Jim Crowley, Elmer Layden, Don Miller, and Harry Stuhldreher, who led Notre Dame to a national championship in 1924.

Rockne was a master innovator of football strategy, and ran the entire Notre Dame program as athletic director and business manager as well as head coach. Unfortunately, he never got a chance to finish out his brilliant career. Knute Rockne died in a plane crash on March 31, 1931, on a flight from Kansas City to Los Angeles, when the plane went down in a field near Bazaar, Kansas. He was inducted into the National Football Foundation Hall of Fame in 1951.

KNUTE ROCKNE ON:

COACHING

"An automobile goes nowhere efficiently, unless it has a quick, hot spark to ignite things, to set the cogs of the machine in motion. So I try to make every player on my team feel he's the spark keeping our machine in motion. On him depends our success and victories."

"A coach's greatest asset is his sense of responsibility—the reliance placed on him by his players. Handling our personnel is the most important phase of coaching. The secret of coaching success can be reduced to a simple formula: strict discipline in your training program and on the field, combined with a high and continuing interest in all your other relationships with your kids."

"Win or lose, I'm running this team. Nobody else has anything to say about its make-up, it's plans, it's type of play. It's my show. If I flop, let 'em pan me. If we're a hit, let 'em say anything they want. I worked hard around here as an assistant for many years, and seldom saw my name in print. Well, all I want now is the truth."

—After taking over as head coach at Notre Dame

DETERMINATION

"Build up your weaknesses until they become your strong points."

FAIRNESS

"Win or lose, do it fairly."

FOOTBALL

"The essence of football was blocking, tackling, and execution based on timing, rhythm, and deception."

"Football is a game played with arms, legs, and shoulders, but mostly from the neck up."

"Four years of football are calculated to breed in the average man more of the ingredients of success in life than almost any academic course he takes."

HOME FIELD

"We use the same boys and the same plays on the road as we do at home. Our execution is expected to be the same. At home we're the hosts, and I never liked the idea of being embarrassed in front of our friends. On the road we're somebody else's guests, and we play in a way that they're not going to forget we visited them."

INTELLIGENCE

"We can all be geniuses because one definition of genius is the infinite capacity for taking pains. Perfection in petty detail is most essential. Generalities don't count and won't help you in football."

"The only qualification[s] for a lineman are to be big and dumb. To be a back, you only have to be dumb."

LOSING

"Show me a good and gracious loser, and I'll show you a failure."

NOTRE DAME

"I don't want anybody going out there to die for dear old Notre Dame. Hell, I want you fighting to stay alive!"

PLAYERS

"I'll find out what my best team is when I find out how many doctors and lawyers and good husbands and good citizens have come off of each and every one of my teams."

PRAYER

"I've found that prayers work best when you have big players."

SPORTSMANSHIP

"One man practicing sportsmanship is better than a hundred teaching it."

TEAMWORK

"No star playing, just football."

"The secret is to work less as individuals and more as a team. As a coach, I play not my 11 best, but my best 11."

THINKING

"Most men, when they think they are thinking, are merely rearranging their prejudices."

WINNING

"When you were riding on the crest of a wave, you were most likely to be missing out on something."

"Winning too often is as disastrous as losing too often. Both get the same results, the falling off of the public's enthusiasm."

"We count on winning. And if we lose, don't beef. And the best way to prevent beefing is—don't lose."

•••

Knute Rockne's "Win One for the Gipper" speech at halftime of the 1928 Army game, as told in the 1940 film, *Knute Rockne—All American*:

"Well, boys...I haven't a thing to say. Played a great game...all of you. Great game. I guess we just can't expect to win 'em all. I'm going to tell you something I've kept to myself for years. None of you ever knew George Gipp. It was long before your time. But you know what a tradition he is at Notre Dame...And the last thing he said to me—'Rock,' he said—'sometime, when the team is up against it—and the breaks are beating the boys—tell them to go out there with all they got and win just one for the Gipper...

"I don't know where I'll be then, Rock,' he said—'but I'll know about it—and I'll be happy.'"

•••

Rockne gave another speech, this one actually recorded for posterity by newsreels in the 1920s, to his Notre Dame players. The date is unclear, but it was most likely in the late 1920s:

"And the same backfield, Jimmy, you and Collins, Chevigny, and Niemiec. Now, the success of any team men is based on team-play—the same as you've shown all year. Sacrifice; unselfish sacrifice! These are the fellows they say are pretty good, but I think we're better! And I think if we get ourselves keyed up to a point, and when we're confident of that...why, the results will take care of themselves.

"All right, now. On the kickoff, if we receive, the zone men will drop back to the receiver and block long, that old Notre Dame style. If we kick off, which the rest of the teams want, let's run down fast, just as fast as you can run. And then we go on defense. And on defense, I want the center in and out of that line, according to the situation. Use your old head! And I want you guards charging through as far as you can go—on every play. Expect the play right over you every time.

"And the tackles—I want you to go in a yard and a half, and then check yourselves. Spread your feet, squat down low, and be ready with your hands and elbows, so you won't be sideswiped. But I want the ends in there fast every play. Every play, but under control. And you men in the backfield there, I want you to analyze it before you move. If they throw a forward pass, a zone pass, wait 'til you see the ball in the air, and then go and get it! And when we get it, boys, that's when we go on offense. And that's when we go to 'em, and, don't forget, we're gonna pick on one last tackle that is weak.

"We're going inside of 'em, we're going outside of 'em! Inside of 'em! Outside of 'em! And when we get them on the run once, we're going to keep 'em on the run. And we're not going to pass unless their secondary comes up too close. But don't forget, men: We're gonna get 'em on the run, we're gonna go, go, go, go! And we aren't going to stop until we go over that goal line! And don't forget, men: Today is the day we're gonna win. They can't lick us—and that's how it goes...The first platoon men—go in there and fight, fight, fight, fight, fight! What do you say, men?"

Sanity

"Well, that's a scoop."

>—*New York Mets manager Bobby Valentine, referring to a comment made by catcher Mike Piazza that pitcher Roger Clemens was unstable*

"Not that I've paid for it."

>—*New York Mets manager Bobby Valentine, when asked if he had ever been psychoanalyzed*

"I plead guilty to assigning Jay Johnstone and Jim Piersall as roommates. It was an easy decision. I didn't want to screw up two rooms."

>—*Oakland Athletics manager Bill Rigney, commenting on two of the most eccentric players in baseball*

"Neil Armstrong brought him back from the moon."

>—*Oakland Athletics manager Bill Rigney on how Jay Johnstone wound on up the Oakland roster*

"There is a thin line between genius and insanity, and in Larry's [MacPhail] case it was sometimes so thin you could see him drifting back and forth."

—Baseball manager Leo Durocher on the intelligence and eccentricities of Brooklyn Dodgers owner Larry MacPhail

"I was with the Yankees the spring that [Mike] Kekich and [Fritz] Peterson switched wives."

—Atlanta Braves manager Bobby Cox when asked if he had ever been through a chaotic spring training before

SCANDAL

"You know what FSU stands for, don't you? Free Shoes University."

—University of Florida football coach Steve Spurrier after his rival, Florida State, was involved in the Foot Locker Scandal (players going on shopping sprees at Foot Locker courtesy of boosters) after its National Championship season

SCHEDULES

"There are a lot of guys who played tough schedules who are working at K-mart."

—Basketball coach George Raveling

SELFISHNESS

"Nothing devastates a football team like a selfish player. It's a cancer."

—Football coach and owner Paul Brown

"You should sub a player out when you see a player not going full-speed or playing selfish basketball."

—North Carolina basketball coach Dean Smith

SELFLESSNESS

"You can never pay back, but you can always pay forward."

—Football coach Woody Hayes

SERVICE

"Do right. Do your best. Treat others as you want to be treated."

—Football coach Lou Holtz

SEX

"We play 162 games. There would be a lot of things weak—probably weak minds—if we started trying to keep guys from doing what is natural."

—New York Mets manager Bobby Valentine when asked if players should not have sex before games to save their strength

SLEEP

"You've got to sleep before you can have nightmares."

—Hockey coach Bep Guidolin

SMOKING

"Economics played a role. Raleighs have gone from $6.50 to $9 a carton, but there's a three-quarter cent coupon on the back. You can get all kinds of things with them, blenders, everything. I saved up enough one time and got Al Bumbry."

—Baseball manager Earl Weaver

"Every time I fail to smoke a cigarette between innings, the opposition will score."

—Baseball manager Earl Weaver

SOUL

"There's nothing that cleanses your soul like getting the hell kicked out of you."

—Football coach Woody Hayes

SPORTSMANSHIP

"Because no visiting team has ever scored 50 points in this stadium and we wanted to be the first."

—Football coach Steve Spurrier telling reporters why he went for a last second passing touchdown in Athens against Georgia while Spurrier's Gators had a huge lead

"Show me a sportsman and I'll show you a player I'm looking to trade."

—Manager Leo Durocher

"Sportsmanship and easygoing methods are all right, but it is the prospect of a hot fight that brings out the crowds."

—New York Giants manager John McGraw

SPORTSWRITERS

"What's the difference between a 3-week-old puppy and a sportswriter? In six weeks, the puppy will stop whining."

—Football coach Mike Ditka

"The Lord taught me to love everybody, but the last ones I learned to love were the sportswriters."

—Baseball manager Alvin Dark

"The best three years of their lives are spent in the third grade."

—Basketball coach George Raveling

SPOUSES

"Because she is too ugly to kiss goodbye."

—NFL coach Bum Phillips when asked why he takes his wife on road trips.

STADIUMS

"Yeah, it was a crummy stadium. We had crud hanging off it. The fans are right on top of everybody. When people came in there, it was hard to beat us."

—Football coach Joe Gibbs on RFK Stadium, the former home of the Washington Redskins

232

STATISTICS

"Say you were standing with one foot in the oven and the other foot in a bucket of ice. According to the percentage people, you should be about perfectly comfortable."

—*Baseball manager Bobby Bragan*

"Games are not won and lost on statistics, they are won and lost on people who make plays."

—*Football coach Tony Sparano*

"Statistics are like loose women...once you get them, you can do anything you want with them."

—*Football coach Walt Michaels*

STRATEGY

"Chuck him [Honus Wagner] the ball as hard as you can and pray."

—*New York Giants manager John McGraw on pitching to Honus Wagner*

"The way to get a ball past Honus [Wagner] is to hit it 8 feet over his head."

—*New York Giants manager John McGraw on another way to play against Wagner*

"You can't sit on a lead and run a few plays into the line and just kill the clock. You've got to throw the ball over the goddamn plate and give the other man his chance. That's why baseball is the greatest game of them all."

—*Baseball manager Earl Weaver*

"I always tried to hit the ball back through the box because that is the largest unprotected area."

—*Manager Roger Hornsby talking about his hitting strategy from his playing days*

"Cobb would have to play center field on my all-time team. But where would that put Speaker? In left. If I had them both, I would certainly play them that way."

—*New York Giants manager John McGraw on how he would use Ty Cobb and Tris Speaker*

"My best game plan is to sit on the bench and call out specific instructions like 'C'mon Boog,' 'Get ahold of one, Frank,' or 'Let's go, Brooks.'"

—*Baseball manager Earl Weaver*

"Why shouldn't we pitch to Babe Ruth? We pitch to better hitters in the National League."

—*New York Giants manager John McGraw on the question of whether or not to pitch to Babe Ruth*

"You don't save a pitcher for tomorrow. Tomorrow it may rain."

—*Baseball manager Leo Durocher*

STRESS

"I think we can win it if my brain holds out."

—*New York Giants manager John McGraw on the pressure of managing in a pennant race.*

SUCCESS

"Today, life is so much more convenient than when I was young. We didn't have TV. We seldom saw an airplane. A lot has changed, but there is one thing in 62 years that I have not seen. I have not seen anyone find a convenient or easy way to succeed at something or to win."

—Football coach Lou Holtz

"Success is not forever and failure is not fatal."

—Football coach Don Shula

"The answer to three questions will determine your success or failure:

1. Can people trust me to do my best?
2. Am I committed to the task in hand?
3. Do I care about other people and show it?

If the answers to all three questions are yes, there is no way you can fail."

—Football coach Lou Holtz

SUPERSTITIONS

"I'm wearing the same socks, shirt, and underwear, too!"

—Baseball manager Leo Durocher on his choice of clothing during a winning streak

National Baseball Hall of Fame Library
Cooperstown, N.Y.

CASEY STENGEL

He was known as "The Old Professor," and rightly so, because Charles Dillon "Casey" Stengel had a Ph.D., not just in baseball, but in life. He ranks among the greatest managers in the history of baseball, but his achievements are sometimes overshadowed by his colorful personality and his legendary quotable style, in a language known as "Stengelese."

His life is a timeline of baseball history for much of the 20th century. Born in 1889 in Kansas City, Missouri, Stengel began his major league baseball career with the Brooklyn Dodgers in the latter part of the 1912 season. He made his presence known right away going 4 for 4 in his first game, a baseball record for an inaugural performance. The young, quirky outfielder was given the nickname Casey, in honor of his hometown, K.C.

Stengel became a standout fielder at Ebbets Field in Brooklyn, playing all three outfield positions. He starred for the Dodgers in the 1916 World Series, batting .364. But before the 1918 season started, Stengel was traded to the Pittsburgh Pirates. He was a platoon player in Pittsburgh, but he was still a fan favorite back in Brooklyn, and cemented his place in Dodger history one Sunday afternoon in 1919 when the Pirates were playing at Ebbets Field. Stengel had gotten a small bird from one of his former teammates in the Brooklyn bullpen. When he came up to hit, he tipped his hat to the crowd and the bird flew out.

Stengel was traded again in 1921, this time back to New York, to the Giants, playing under manager John McGraw. He played on three National League pennant-winning teams from 1921 through 1923, and hit two game-winning home runs in the 1923 series for the Giants. One was an inside-the-park home run in the first game with two outs in the ninth inning, running around the bases as one of his shoes was falling off him. He was traded after the season to the Boston Braves, and finished his playing career there in 1925. He had played in 1,277 games, with a .284 batting average.

Stengel then embarked on the part of his baseball career that would put him in the Hall of Fame: managing, though for a long time it didn't seem that Stengel would go down in history as one of the all-time great managers. He got a job managing the minor league Toledo Mud Hens in 1926, but was out of a job by 1931 when the team went bankrupt. He found his way back to the major leagues and Brooklyn when he was hired as a coach for the Dodgers in 1931. Two years later, he took over for Dodgers manager Max Carey, but Stengel would meet with frustrating failure, finishing sixth, fifth, and seventh, and he was fired after the 1936 season.

Two years later he managed to land another major league managing job, this time with the Boston Braves. But again, from 1938 through 1943, his team never finished higher than fifth place, and he was fired in the spring of 1944. Stengel was forced to return to managing in the minor leagues, and it looked as if his major league managing career, at the age of 55, was over. But after stints with the Milwaukee Brewers and Kansas City in the American Association, Stengel landed the minor league job that would be his salvation. He took over the Oakland Oaks in the Pacific Coast League in 1946 and led them to a second place finish the first year and first place in 1948. The general manager who hired Stengel in Oakland was George Weiss, who moved on to run the New York Yankees. When the Yankees fired Bucky Harris after the 1948 season, Weiss hired Stengel, a move that met with criticism, given his reputation as a clown and a losing manager.

But Stengel was the right man at the right time, and he led the Yankees to a World Series championship in his first season in New York in 1949. Stengel led the Yankees to four more consecutive World Championships, a record not only for World Championships, but even for pennants. Before he was done with the Yankees after 1960, Stengel had a remarkable record of 10 pennants and seven World Championships. He managed such great players as Mickey Mantle, Yogi Berra, and Whitey Ford, and had a knack of knowing when to use the right player in a platoon situation. But after the Yankees lost to the Pittsburgh Pirates after the seventh game of the 1960 World Series, Stengel, along with Weiss, was fired. Stengel, at the age of 70, was considered too old.

He had one last hurrah, though, in his baseball career, and this managing stint, like his earlier days, was filled with losing teams. However, it did nothing to diminish Stengel's legacy, and when he took over the job as manager of the expansion New York Mets, it only enhanced his popularity and added to the Stengel lore. The Mets were the worst team in major league baseball history that first year, with a 40-120 record, but the focus was on Stengel much of the time, as he used his "Stengelese" to ease the pain of losing for New York fans and entertain them. He was forced to retire halfway through the 1965 season, when he broke his hip before his 75th birthday. With a career winning managing record of 1,926-1,867 (37-26 in World Series games), Stengel retired and went back to working as a bank officer in Glendale, Calif., with a sign on his desk that said, "Stengelese Spoken Here." He died on September 29, 1975, but left behind a library of Stengelese.

CASEY STENGEL ON:

AGE

"I'll never make the mistake of being 70 again."

"Most people my age are dead at the present time, and you could look it up."

"If anyone wants me, tell them I'm being embalmed."

"There comes a time in every man's life, and I've had plenty of them."

"You can't go out to the mound, hobbling, and take a pitcher out with a cane."

"Old timers' games, weekends, and airplane landings are alike. If you can walk away from them, they're successful."

AUTOGRAPHS

"I love signing autographs. I'll sign anything but veal cutlets. My pen slips on veal cutlets."

BASEBALL

"Can't anybody here play this game?"

"Good pitching will always stop good hitting and vice-versa."

"Well, that's baseball. Rags to riches one day and riches to rags the next. But I've been in it 36 years and I'm used to it."

CATCHING

"You have to have a catcher or you'll have all passed balls."

DRINKING

"Don't drink in the hotel bar, that's where I do my drinking."

"I came in here and a fella asked me to have a drink. I said, 'I don't drink.' Then another fella said, 'Hear you and Joe DiMaggio aren't speaking,' and I said, 'I'll take that drink.'"

"They say some of my stars drink whiskey, but I have found that ones who drink milkshakes don't win many ball games."

EFFORT

"All I ask is that you bust your hiney on that field."

FRIENDS

"It's wonderful to meet so many friends that I didn't used to like."

GEOGRAPHY

"They brought me up with the Brooklyn Dodgers, which at the time, was in Brooklyn."

HEALTH

"My health is good enough about the shoulders."

"Wake up muscles, we're in New York now."

HITTING

"I was such a dangerous hitter I even got intentional walks in batting practice."

HONORS

"I feel greatly honored to have a ballpark named after me, especially since I've been thrown out of so many."

LANGUAGE

"People ask me, 'Casey, how can you speak so much when you don't talk English too good?' Well, I've been invited to Europe, and I say, 'They don't speak English over there too.'"

LEFT-HANDERS

"Left-handers have more enthusiasm for life. They sleep on the wrong side of the bed, and their head gets more stagnant on that side."

LOSING

"Most ball games are lost, not won."

"Been in this game 100 years, but I see new ways to lose 'em I never knew existed before."

"Don't cut my throat, I may want to do that later myself."

MANAGING

"The secret of managing is to keep the guys who hate you away from the guys who are undecided."

MISTAKES

"I don't like them fellas who drive in two runs and let in three."

MONEY

"You have to go broke three times to learn how to make a living."

"You say to the youth of America, 'Here is the opportunity,' and the youth of America says, 'How much are you going to pay me?'"

NEW YORK METS

"The only thing worse than a Mets game is a Mets double-header."

"The Mets have shown me more ways to lose than I even knew existed."

"We [the Mets] are a much improved ball club, now we lose in extra innings!"

"He [Lyndon B. Johnson] wanted to see poverty, so he came to see my team ['64 Mets]."

"We've ['62 Mets] got to learn to stay out of triple plays."

"The Mets are gonna be amazing."

"This club ['69 Mets] plays better baseball now. Some of them look fairly alert."

OWNERS

"If you're playing ball and thinking about managing, you're crazy. You'd be better off thinking about being an owner. It's safer."

PITCHERS

"I mighta been able to make it as a pitcher except for one thing: I had a rather awkward motion and every time I brought my left arm forward I hit myself in the ear."

"I don't know if he throws a spitball, but he sure spits on the ball."

"It's high time something was done for the pitchers. They put up the stands and take down fences to make more home runs and plague the pitchers. Let them revive the spitter and help the pitchers make a living."

"Nobody ever had too many of them [pitchers]."

"Aim the ball right at the middle of the plate, because you couldn't hit anything you aim at and maybe you will catch a corner."

—Advising pitcher Tracy Stallard

PLAYERS

"He [Babe Ruth] was very brave at the plate. You rarely saw him fall away from a pitch. He stayed right in there. No one drove him out."

"He'd [Yogi Berra] fall in a sewer and come up with a gold watch."

"He [Gil Hodges] fields better on one leg than anybody else I got on two."

"Amazing strength, amazing power—he [Ron Swoboda] can grind the dust out of the bat. He will be great, super, even wonderful. Now, if he can only learn to catch a fly ball."

"He [Mickey Mantle] should lead the league in everything. With his combination of speed and power he should win the triple batting crown every year. In fact, he should do anything he wants to do."

"I got players with bad watches—they can't tell midnight from noon."

"He [Satchel Paige] threw the ball as far from the bat and as close to the plate as possible."

"I couldna done it without my players."

"Kid [Phil Rizzuto] you're too small. You ought to go out and shine shoes."

"Look at him [Bobby Richardson]—he doesn't drink, he doesn't smoke, he doesn't chew, he doesn't stay out late, and he still can't hit .250."

"No, even my players aren't players."

"[Roger] Hornsby could run like anything but not like this kid. Cobb was the fastest I ever saw for being sensational on the bases..."

"They say he's [Yogi Berra] funny. Well, he has a lovely wife and family, a beautiful home, money in the bank, and he plays golf with millionaires. What's funny about that?"

"I knew he couldn't hit, but no one told me he couldn't catch, either."

—*Talking about New York Mets catcher Chris Cannizzaro*

SIZE

"All right, everyone, line up alphabetically according to your height."

STRATEGY

"I always heard it couldn't be done, but sometimes it don't always work."

TALENT

"As great as the other men were on the ball club, there comes a time when you get a weakness and it might be physical."

"Mister, that boy couldn't hit the ground if he fell out of an airplane."

"Son, we'd like to keep you around this season but we're going to try and win a pennant."

"That kid can hit balls over buildings."

WALKING

"If you walk backwards, you'll find out that you can go forward and people won't know if you're coming or going."

WINNING

"If this keeps up [four game winning streak] I'm about to manage until I'm a hundred."

"If we're going to win the pennant, we've got to start thinking we're not as good as we think we are."

"The Yankees don't pay me to win every day, just two out of three."

"You got to get 27 outs to win."

WOMEN

"Being with a woman all night never hurt no professional baseball player. It's staying up all night looking for a woman that does him in."

"If you don't get it by midnight, chances are you ain't gonna get it, and if you do, it ain't worth it."

WHAT OTHERS HAVE SAID ABOUT CASEY STENGEL:

"Casey knew his baseball. He only made it look like he was fooling around. He knew every move that was ever invented and some that we haven't even caught on to yet."

—*Baseball manager Sparky Anderson*

"I'm probably the only guy who worked for Stengel before and after he was a genius."

—*Pitcher Warren Spahn*

"I never saw a man who juggled his lineup so much and who played as many hunches so successfully."

—*Baseball owner and manager Connie Mack*

•••

In 1958, Casey Stengel testified at the U.S. Senate Anti-Trust and Monopoly Subcommittee hearings and gave what may have been the most memorable and confusing testimony ever given by anyone in the sports and entertainment industry in the country. Here are some excerpts from that appearance:

"Well, I started in professional ball in 1910. I have been in professional ball, I would say, for 48 years. I have been employed by numerous ball clubs in the majors and in the minor leagues. I started in the minor leagues with Kansas City. I played as low as class D ball, which was at Shelbyville, Ky., and also class C ball, and class A ball, and I have advanced in baseball as a ballplayer.

"I had many years that I was not so successful as a ballplayer, as it is a game of skill. And then I was no doubt discharged by baseball in which I had to go back to the minor leagues as a manager, and after being in the minor leagues as a manager, I became a major league manager in several cities and was discharged, we call it 'discharged,' because there is no question I had to leave. [Laughter]. And I returned to the minor leagues at Milwaukee, Kansas City, and Oakland, Calif., and then returned to the major leagues.

"In the last 10 years, naturally, in major league baseball with the New York Yankees, the New York Yankees have had tremendous success, and while I am not the ballplayer who does the work, I have no doubt worked for a ball club that is very capable in the office. I must have splendid ownership, I must have very capable men who are in radio and television, which is no doubt you know that we have mentioned the three names—you will say they are very great.

"We have a wonderful press that follows us. Anybody should in New York City, where you have so many million people. Our ball club has been successful because we have it, and we have the spirit of 1776. We put it into the ball field and if you are not capable of becoming a great ballplayer since I have been in as a manager, in 10 years, you are notified that if you don't produce on the ball field, the salary that you receive, we will allow you to be traded to play and give your services to other clubs.

"The great proof was yesterday. Three of the young men that were stars and picked by the players in the American League to be in the All-Star game were Mr. Cerv, who is at Kansas City; Mr. Jensen, who was at Boston; and I might say Mr. Triandos that caught for the Baltimore ball club, all three of those players were my members and to show you I was not such a brilliant manager they got away from me and were chosen by the players and I was fortunate enough to have them come back to play where I was successful as a manager.

"If I have been in baseball for 48 years there must be some good in it. I was capable and strong enough at one time to do any kind of work but I came back to baseball and I have been in baseball ever since. I have been up and down the ladder. I know there are some things in baseball, 35 to 50 years ago, that are better now than they were in those days. In those days, my goodness, you could not transfer a ball club in the minor leagues, class D, class C ball, class A ball. How could you transfer a ball club when you did not have a highway? How could you transfer a ball club when the railroads then would take you to a town you got off and then you had to wait and sit up five hours to go to another ball club?

"How could you run baseball then without night ball? You had to have night ball to improve the proceeds to pay larger salaries and I went to work, the first year I received $135 a month. I thought that was amazing. I had to put away enough money to go to dental college. I found out it was not better in dentistry, I stayed in baseball.

"Any other questions you would like to ask me? I want to let you know that as to the legislative end of baseball you men will have to consider that what you are here for. I am a bench manager. I will speak about anything from the playing end—in the major or minor leagues—and do anything I can to help you.

Senator Kefauver: "Mr. Stengel, are you prepared to answer particularly why baseball wants this bill passed?

Mr. Stengel: "Well, I would have to say at the present time, I think that baseball has advanced in this respect for the player help. That is an amazing statement for me to make, because you can retire with an annuity at 50 and what organization in America allows you to retire at 50 and receive money?

"I want to further state that I am not a ballplayer, that is, put into that pension fund committee. At my age, and I have been in baseball, well, I say I am possibly the oldest man who is working in baseball. I would say that when they start an annuity for the ballplayers to better their conditions, it should have been done, and I think it has been done. I think it should be the way they have done it, which is a very good thing.

"The reason they possibly did not take the managers in at that time was because radio and television or the income to ball clubs was not large enough that you could have put in a pension plan. Now, I am not a member of the pension plan. You have young men here who are, who represent the ball clubs. They represent them as players and since I am not a member and don't receive pension from a fund which you think, my goodness, he ought to be declared in that too, but I would say that is a great thing for the ballplayers. That is one thing I will say for the ballplayers, they have an advanced pension fund. I should think it was gained by radio and television or you could not have enough money to pay anything of that type.

"Now the second thing about baseball that I think is very interesting to the public or to all of us that it is the owner's fault if he does not improve his club, along with the officials in the ball club and the players.

"Now what causes that? If I am going to go on the road and we are a traveling ball club and you know the cost of transportation now—we travel sometimes with three Pullman coaches, the New York Yankees, and remember I am just a salaried man and do not own stock in the New York Yankees, I found out that in traveling with the New York Yankees on the road and all, that it is the best, and we have broken records in Washington this year, we have broken them in every city but New York and we have lost two clubs that have gone out of the city of New York.

"Of course, we have had some bad weather, I would say that they are mad at us in Chicago, we fill the parks. They have come out to see good material. I will say they are mad at us in Kansas City, but we broke their attendance record.

"Now on the road we only get possibly 27 cents. I am not positive of these figures, as I am not an official. If you go back 15 years or if I owned stock in the club I would give them to you.

Senator Kefauver: "Mr. Stengel, I am not sure that I made my question clear. [Laughter.]

Mr. Stengel: "Yes, sir. Well that is all right. I am not sure I am going to answer yours perfectly either. [Laughter.]"

TALENT

"If you don't have outstanding relief pitching, you might as well piss on the fire and call the dogs."

—Baseball manager Whitey Herzog

"More than anyone else, he's [Hank Aaron] made me wish I wasn't a manager."

—Baseball manager Walt Alston

"The only way we could have [stopped him] was to have shot him before the game started."

—Hockey coach Brian Sutter on trying to stop Jaromir Jagr

"Mathewson was the greatest pitcher who ever lived. He had knowledge, judgment, perfect control, and form. It was wonderful to watch him pitch when he wasn't pitching against you."

—Philadelphia Athletics owner and manager Connie Mack, talking about pitcher Christy Mathewson

"We have 44 defenses for him, but he has 45 ways to score."

—*Basketball coach Al Attles on defending
guard Nate Archibald*

"Attaway to hit, George."

—*Kansas City Royals manager Jim Frey describing
the hitting advice he offers to Jim Frey*

"Nobody ever won a pennant without a star shortstop."

—*Baseball manager Leo Durocher*

"Having Willie Stargell on your ball club is like having a
diamond ring on your finger."

—*Pittsburgh Pirates manager Chuck Tanner*

"What else can you say about Wayne Gretzky? Seventeen
years of this. That's why he's the greatest player that ever
played the game. He showed us his stuff tonight and give
him credit for that. That's why he's Wayne Gretzky."

—*Florida hockey coach Doug MacLean after Gretzky
scored a playoff hat trick against the Panthers*

"Let him [Ty Cobb] sleep if he will. If you get him riled up,
he will annihilate us."

—*Philadelphia Athletics owner
and manager Connie Mack*

"In my prime, I think I could have handled Michael Jordan.
Of course, he would only be 12 years old."

—*Basketball coach Jerry Sloan*

"He [Honus Wagner] was the nearest thing to a perfect player no matter where his manager chose to play him."

>—*New York Giants baseball manager John McGraw on the talent of Honus Wagner*

"As one of nine men, DiMaggio is the best player that ever lived."

>—*Philadelphia Athletic baseball owner and manager Connie Mack declaring that Joe DiMaggio was the greatest player in the history of the game*

"John Elway is an immediate cure for coach's burnout."

>—*Football coach John Madden*

"I don't like to sound egotistical, but every time I stepped up to the plate with a bat in my hands, I couldn't help but feel sorry for the pitcher."

>—*Baseball manager Roger Hornsby, talking about his hitting prowess as a player*

"If I had all the men I've ever handled and they were in their prime and there was one game I wanted to win above all others, Albert [Chief Bender] would be my man."

>—*Philadelphia Athletics owner and manager Connie Mack espousing his faith in Chief Bender*

"Earl may not be in a class by himself, but whatever class he's in, it doesn't take long to call the roll."

>—*Football coach Bum Phillips on running back Earl Campbell*

"[Ty] Cobb is all wet. He talks about a game which had no night play, a game in which the pitcher had everything his own way. He could apply saliva, tobacco juice, mud, talcum powder, or a file to the ball. He could load it with phonograph needles, raise the seams and do anything else he wished with it. And a ball remained in play until it was ready to break apart. Now the advantage is all with the hitters."

*—Baseball manager Roger Hornsby on Ty Cobb's
claim to be the greatest ballplayer of all time*

"We need just two players to be a contender. Just Babe Ruth and Sandy Koufax."

*—Baseball manager Whitey Herzog
on his team's lack of talent*

"An outfield composed of Cobb, Speaker, and Ruth, even with Ruth, lacks the combined power of DiMaggio, Musial, and [Ted] Williams."

*—Philadelphia Athletics owner and manager Connie
Mack comparing the great outfielders of different eras*

"My mother could have managed Barry Bonds. That's how good he is."

—Pittsburgh Pirates manager Jim Leyland

"Without Ernie Banks, the Cubs would finish on Albuquerque."

—Baseball manager Jimmy Dykes

"He [Sandy Koufax] throws a 'radio ball,' a pitch you hear, but you don't see."

—Baseball manager Gene Mauch

"Play him [Richie Allen], fine him, and play him again."

*—Baseball manager Gene Mauch on how to handle the
talented but troublesome Richie Allen*

"The coach who thinks his coaching is more important than his talent is an idiot."

—Basketball coach Joe Lapchick

"You got a hundred more young kids than you have a place for on your club. Every one of them has had a going away party. They have been given the shaving kit and the $50. They kissed everybody and said, 'See you in the majors in two years.' You see these poor kids who shouldn't be there in the first place. You write on the report card '4-4-4 and out.' That's the lowest rating in everything. Then you call 'em in and say, 'It's the consensus among us that we're going to let you go back home.' Some of them cry, some get mad, but none of them will leave until you answer them one question, 'Skipper, what do you think?' And you gotta look every one of those kids in the eye and kick their dreams in the ass and say no. If you say it mean enough, maybe they do themselves a favor and don't waste years learning what you can see in a day. They don't have what it takes to make the majors, just like I never had it."

—Baseball manager Earl Weaver

TEACHING

"When someone asks me what time it is, I always want to tell them how to build a watch."

—Hockey coach Herb Brooks

TEAMS

"You sweat out the free agent thing in November then you make the trades in December. Then you struggle to sign the guys left in January, and in February I get down to sewing all the new numbers on the uniforms."

—Baseball manager Whitey Herzog

"I have a good feeling about this club. But that could be gas."

—Cleveland Indians manager Mike Hargrove on his team's chances of going to the 1998 American League Championship Series

"You win pennants in the off-season when you build your teams with trades and free agents."

—Baseball manager Earl Weaver

"We have too many Marys and not enough Williams."

—Lou Holtz, shortly after taking over as head coach of the College of William and Mary

"What we're trying to do here is make chicken salad out of chicken s---."

—Washington Senators baseball manager Joe Kuhel

TEAMWORK

"Individual grievances and pet peeves have got to go by the wayside. Generally, you don't have to worry about the guys who are playing every day, it's the guys who are sitting on the bench that are the ones that get needles in their pants."

—Los Angeles Dodgers manager Walt Alston

"It's amazing how much can be accomplished if no one cares about who gets the credit."

—Football coach Blanton Collier

"We can't play stupid hockey, dumb hockey, greedy hockey, selfish hockey. We have to put the team ahead of our personal feelings."

—Tampa Bay hockey coach Terry Crisp

"A team equals a fist, not five fingers."

—Duke basketball coach Mike Krzyzewski

"Great teamwork is the only way we create the breakthroughs that define our careers."

—Basketball coach Pat Riley

"A star can win any game; a team can win every game."

—Basketball coach and television analyst Jack Ramsay

"On a good team there are no superstars. There are great players who show they are great players by being able to play with others as a team. They have the ability to be superstars, but if they fit into a good team, they make sacrifices, they do things necessary to help the team win. What the numbers are in salaries or statistics don't matter; how they play together does."

—New York Knicks basketball coach Red Holzman

"The glory of sport is witnessing a well-coached team perform as a single unit, striving for a common goal and ultimately bringing distinction to the jersey the players represent."

—Basketball coach and television analyst Dick Vitale

"The strength of the team is each individual member; the strength of each member is the team."

—Basketball coach Phil Jackson

TEMPER

"Temper is something the good Lord gave me and I just can't throw it out the window."

—Baseball manager Billy Martin

THINKING

"A slick way to outfigure a person is to get him figuring you figure he's figuring you're figuring he'll figure you aren't really figuring what you want him to figure you figure."

—Baseball manager Whitey Herzog

"Thinking about the devil is worse than seeing the devil."

—Baseball manager and general manager Branch Rickey

TIES

"A tie is like kissing your sister."

—Michigan State football coach Duffy Daugherty

"Everybody says a tie is like kissing your sister. I guess it's better than kissing your brother."

—Football coach Lou Holtz

TRADES

"Trade a player a year too early rather than a year too late."

—Baseball manager and general manager Branch Rickey

Mitchell Layton

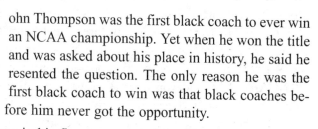

JOHN THOMPSON

J ohn Thompson was the first black coach to ever win an NCAA championship. Yet when he won the title and was asked about his place in history, he said he resented the question. The only reason he was the first black coach to win was that black coaches before him never got the opportunity.

Even in his finest moment, John Thompson never lost the perspective of the world around him, and that is what has always made him an important person to listen to. His words always carry the weight of perspective.

Thompson was born on September 2, 1941, in Washington D.C. He grew tall (eventually to 6-foot 10-inches) and his presence dominated high school basketball in Washington for four years with Archbishop John Carroll High School. He was a high school All-American in 1960, and led his school to two city championships. Thompson went on to play college basketball at Providence, where he also starred as an All-American and Most Valuable Player in his senior year in 1964. He joined the Boston Celtics in 1964 and played as the backup center to the legendary Bill Russell on two NBA championship teams in 1965 and 1966.

But Thompson's greatness did not come as a player. His personality and intelligence had him pegged as a leader in basketball: a coach. After leaving the NBA, he began his coaching career with St. Anthony's High back home in Washington, and from 1966 to 1971 his teams compiled a 122-28 record.

His record landed him a job in college, trying to turn around the Georgetown University basketball program in Washington, which had fallen on hard times with a 3-23 record the season before Thompson took over. He not only turned the program around, he made Georgetown a national power and one of the most popular college teams in the country. From 1972 until he resigned in 1999, Thompson had a record of 596-239. His teams appeared in three Final Fours (1982, 1984, 1985), played in 14 consecutive NCAA tournaments (1979-1992), made 24 consecutive post-season appearances (20 NCAA, 4 NIT) and won seven Big East Tournament championships. His national championship came against Houston in 1984. Thompson was also an assistant coach on the 1976 Olympic gold medal basketball team and head coach of the 1988 bronze-medal-winning squad.

Along the way, Thompson won seven Coach of the Year awards: Big East (1980, 1987, 1992), United States Basketball Writers Association and The Sporting News (1984), National Association of Basketball Coaches (1985), and United Press International (1987). He coached a number of players who went on to become NBA stars, including Patrick Ewing, Alonzo Mourning, Dikembe Mutombo, and Allen Iverson.

Throughout his coaching career, Thompson was an outspoken critic of injustices he found within the college sports system, and his willingness to speak his mind has served him well in his post-coaching life. He has a sports talk show on WTEM Sportstalk

980 in Washington and is also an NBA analyst for TNT sports. People want to hear what John Thompson has to say.

JOHN THOMPSON ON:

ATHLETICS

"We Americans use our sports, we use our religion, as fantasies. Those are supposed to be places in which we can escape into a fantasy world. And the reality of those worlds generally hurts us because we are accustomed to using them for psychological refuge. When an athletic figure cites racism, we become very offended because we don't want racism in our sports to be brought up. We want fun!"

AUTHORITY

"I'm not into that business of being relevant to kids. I'm not playing on their team. They're playing on mine. We have certain ways of acting here. My kids are not going to come in here and say, 'Hey baby.' It doesn't make you less of a man to have respect for people."

COACHING

"I've been told I don't have fun. But I enjoy basketball and watching game film and doing what we do at Georgetown. I'm me. And I express who I am with my coaching."

"One of my greatest memories of Boston was Red Auerbach. He was a man I played for that emphasized defense. Red Auerbach was before his time, and his time hasn't come."

"We cover the full court for 40 minutes, and that brings about and creates frustrations in ourselves and in other people at times."

"I created a situation where I could succeed and make them need me."

COMPASSION

"You know, I got a lot of letters criticizing me over the years, but I've gotten so much mail about that one vision of me with my arm around Freddie Brown. And you know, no one even knows what I said to him. I could have been saying, 'You stupid jerk.' I thought that was pretty funny."

—*Speaking of the image of himself consoling Georgetown guard Freddie Brown after he mistakenly passed the ball to North Carolina's James Worthy in the closing seconds of the 1982 NCAA title game*

"I'm his brother."

—*Trying to get into the intensive care unit of a hospital to see* Washington Post *reporter Mark Asher. Thompson is 6 ft. 10 in. tall and black. Asher is 5 ft. 7 in. tall and white.*

COMPETITION

"We used to beat DeMatha for exercise."

—*Talking about his high school playing days at John Carroll High School and their rivalry with DeMatha High School*

DEDICATION

"We play hard, people expect us to do that, and I expect we will continue to do that."

—*Talking about his team's relentless style of play*

DISCIPLINE

"To teach anything, you must have order. To have order, you must have discipline. That means rules that are enforced. But we have torn down any form of accountability for our children. These days, you almost have to go to court to get in a child's face. And some of these kids need somebody in their face. Adults feel they have to apologize for being authority figures. People say the teachers are not dedicated. That's not true. They're afraid. Their hands are tied. They feel like they need an attorney."

EDUCATION

"We now give the impression that an education has no value because a kid can get a $3 million contract if he leaves early...I don't see how anyone can tolerate that education is unimportant. The most dangerous person in the world is the uneducated one. And when people associate him with his race, it's scary."

"Universities are put here to fit the needs of society, not to fulfill their reputation. If the strong can't help the weak, who can?"

"We have an educational problem in this country, and I'm sick and tired of people focusing in on athletes as if that's the only place there's a problem. Athletics just reflect a small part of our society. The kids that we have that are participating in athletics come out of society as a whole. I'm sick about all this bull about athletics being looked at educationally. That's a bunch of hypocrisy."

GAMBLING

"If you illegalize [college sports] gambling in Nevada...you're not going to stop it. We need to learn how to monitor it, learn how to deal with it. If you take [gambling on college sports] out of Las Vegas, every illegal bookie in this country will still be running books, and every kid that has no supervision will be vulnerable to it."

HALL OF FAME

"It's the period to end all sentences whispered about me, John Thompson is in the Hall of Fame, and nobody can ever take that away."

—*Talking about his 1999 election into the Basketball Hall of Fame*

JOY

"The biggest thing that leaps out in my mind is all of the people, particularly of my race, who I felt never had an opportunity to experience what I have."

—*Speaking to reporters after Georgetown's win over Houston in the 1984 NCAA championship game*

LOVE

"You never forget the ones that loved you and cared for you and made all things possible. We didn't have much, but we had an essential ingredient—love for each other."

MONEY

"I think more change has come about because of economics, because people totally disregard color barriers if you have economic value."

"Put yourself in a position of power where you create a need for yourself that has an economic effect on somebody."

"The world is not black or white as much as it is green. And I think our kids have got to understand and learn that."

PERSONALITY

"I'm not Mr. Nice Guy."

"By nature I've always been a suspicious person. I don't trust a lot of people."

"I'm not going to win many popularity contests. I don't have to explain myself. I don't do things for other people. The people who know me know the way I am. I think sometimes my friends feel they have to explain or apologize for me. That's unfortunate. I don't see the need for that, but I feel affectionate toward them for doing it."

PRESSURE

"At times I've been obsessed by the national championship, I've awakened in the middle of the night in the summer saying 'national championship.' Now I have one. I don't want 10 like John Wooden, I just wanted to get one."

—Reacting to the pressure released by winning the NCAA title in 1984

"I know what's happening out there. Every coach of every team we play is saying, 'Georgetown is the greatest team ever put on the face of the earth. No way we can beat them.' Then, if they win, they get twice the credit and if they lose they get no blame. That's called 'fattening frogs for snakes.'"

PUBLIC OPINION

"I can't let my actions be predicated on how I'm perceived. I've got to have something real."

"My life has been written about from a racial standpoint, from a personal standpoint, from an athletic standpoint, from a public standpoint, from a private standpoint, almost from everything since I was 14 years old. I try to consider the source. If I can live with myself, I'm not going to lose a lot of sleep over some strange guy who never talked to me one time in his life. You let the people you respect be the guide."

"Most people don't know you. They try to judge you based on sound bites out of your life. I've never been one to let people know much about me as a person, and at Georgetown, it wasn't necessary. We didn't have doors open. We had the windows taped up."

RACE

"Dr. King didn't do what he did so that I could be free from whites and a slave to blacks. He wanted me to be free. Free to choose and to make my mistakes."

"Society made us racial. I hate to use the word 'racist' because we all get very nervous when people start talking about racism. But society has made us racial. But you have to constantly be in that struggle of being able to deal with that. That's the struggle that society has caused, and that's why these kinds of conversations are extremely important. The racial composition of my team—whites will come to you and say, because my team is predominantly black, that you're a racist. Well, I'm an Uncle Tom to blacks; I'm a racist, and, you know, and I'm going to tell you something. I'm going to tell you something. I don't give a damn what either side says."

"Whether the kid is black, white, green or whatever, I'm not going to sit down with anybody and demean myself by trying to explain myself and justify myself. I'm not going to do that because some ignorant person said I'm prejudiced."

"I'm not interested in apologizing for being a black man. I am as proud as I can be of that. And I believe that you don't put yourself in a situation where you get respect from people if you don't respect yourself. That is very important for me."

"It is much easier to discriminate against blacks in sports than it is to discriminate for them."

"What is implied by the question is a great big blank before the first one came along. And that's a lie. Plenty of other black coaches could have won an NCAA national championship if they had ever had the opportunity. It's not the brains and talent that were missing until I came along. Those have always been there."

RESPECT

"It's not just athletes. It's about more than that. We've allowed children to grow up with no respect. For themselves or anybody else. You know where we are now? We've got kids on the streets with no respect even for life. My life. Their life. They'll kill you. Or be killed. In that moment of anger, they don't care."

TEAMWORK

"You are not going to win with the kids who are just All-Americans. The kids must have more than status, they must have togetherness."

WHAT OTHERS HAVE SAID ABOUT JOHN THOMPSON:

"John Thompson is a rare motivator, a very intelligent person who could lead men and get tremendous respect for himself from his team."

—Former North Carolina basketball coach Dean Smith

"When a kid comes to John, he stops thinking he knows everything, because John lets them know when he's recruiting them that they are going to play how he wants them to play. John is big, loud, and he ain't the prettiest. He lets them know he sets the rules. When those kids are with John, they don't think any further up their body than their big toe. He does all the thinking. He is in charge."

—Former University of the District of Columbia basketball coach Wil Jones

"I've heard John say, and I think it's true, how amazed he is that in America, supposedly founded on individual freedoms, people want to deny him the right to be who he is. He dares to be different in a world of sameness. That, more than anything, is why I respect this man."

—Former University of Southern California basketball coach George Raveling

Umpires

"I made a game effort to argue, but two things were against me: the umpires and the rules."

> —*Baseball manager Leo Durocher*
> *on trying to argue with umpires*

"You know Italians and hand gestures. I had one too many hand gestures."

> —*New York Mets manager Bobby Valentine after*
> *getting thrown out of a game for arguing*

"I never questioned the integrity of an umpire. Their eyesight, yes."

> —*Baseball manager Leo Durocher on his problems with umpires*

"I just don't have that first step explosion anymore."

> —*Baseball manager Lou Piniella, talking about*
> *tripping on the dugout steps and falling*
> *on his way out to argue a call*

"In the olden days, the umpire didn't have to take any courses in mind reading. The pitcher told you he was going to throw at you."

> —*Baseball manager Leo Durocher on umpires*
> *determining intent on pitchers throwing at hitters*

"The first guy who lays a finger on this blind old man is fined 50 bucks."

—Baseball manager Gene Mauch yelling as his players ran on the field to argue an umpire's call

"You argue with the umpire because there is nothing else you can do about it."

—Baseball manager Leo Durocher on why he bothered to argue with umpires

"The job of arguing with the umpire belongs to the manager, because it won't hurt the team if he gets thrown out of the game."

—Baseball manager Earl Weaver

UNDERACHIEVING

"Each of us has been put on earth with the ability to do something well. We cheat ourselves and the world if we don't use that ability as best we can."

—NFL coach George Allen

UNIFORMS

"Hey, I'm just glad to have a uniform."

—Kansas City Royals manager Tony Muser when asked about the Royals new 2002 uniforms. One month into the season, he didn't have one anymore—he was fired.

"Baseball people, and that includes myself, are slow to change and accept new ideas. I remember that it took years to persuade them to put numbers on uniforms."

—Baseball manager and general manager Branch Rickey

Values

"Humanity is the keystone that holds nations and men together. When that collapses, the whole structure crumbles. This is as true of baseball teams as any other pursuit in life."

—Philadelphia Athletics owner
and manager Connie Mack

Winning

"Before you can win, you have to believe you are worthy."

—Football coach Mike Ditka

"In playing or managing, the game of ball is only fun for me when I'm out in front and winning. I don't give a hill of beans for the rest of the game."

—New York Giants manager John McGraw

"A life of frustration is inevitable for any coach whose main enjoyment is winning."

—Pittsburgh Steelers football coach Chuck Noll

"Everything looks nicer when you win. The girls are prettier. The cigars taste better. The trees are greener."

—Baseball manager Billy Martin

"What are we out at the park for, except to win?"

—Baseball manager Leo Durocher

"You can't win them all."

—*Philadelphia Athletics owner and manager Connie Mack*

"Once you start keeping score, winning's the bottom line. It's the American concept."

—*Basketball coach Al McGuire*

"If you don't win, you're going to be fired. If you do win, you've only put off the day you're going to be fired."

—*Baseball manager Leo Durocher*

"Winning is only half of it. Having fun winning is the other half."

—*Football coach Bum Phillips*

"There are 50 games a year when you beat the crap out of them, and there's 50 games a year when they beat the crap out of you. The rest are swing games. You've got to win those games if you are going to win."

—*Kansas City Royals manager Tony Muser*

"Win any way you can as long as you can get away with it."

—*Baseball manager Leo Durocher*

"The main idea is to win."

—*New York Giants manager John McGraw*

"I've always played hard. If that's rough and tough, I can't help it. I don't believe there's any such thing as a good loser. I wouldn't sit down and play a game of cards with you right now without wanting to win. If I hadn't felt that way I wouldn't have got very far in baseball."

—*Baseball manager Roger Hornsby*

"In all the research you do as a coach, studying other coaches and championship-type situations, you find that all those teams combined talent with great defense. You've got to stop other teams to win."

>—*Basketball coach Pat Riley*

"How you play the game is for college ball. When you're playing for money, winning is the only thing that matters."

>—*Baseball manager Leo Durocher*

"My hardest job is to convince the people of Nebraska that 10-1 is not a losing season."

>—*Nebraska football coach Tom Osborne*
>*on the pressure of winning at Nebraska*

"I come to win."

>—*Baseball manager Leo Durocher*

"Parity is not the American way. The American way is to dominate somebody else."

>—*Baseball manager Davey Johnson*

"It's hard to win a pennant, but it's harder to lose one."

>—*Baseball manager Chuck Tanner*

"I'd rather win two or three, lose one, win two or three more. I'm a great believer in things evening out. If you win a whole bunch in a row, somewhere along the line you're going to lose some too."

>—*Los Angeles Dodgers manager Walt Alston*

"The greatest feeling in the world is to win a major league game. The second greatest feeling is to lose a major league game."

>—*Baseball manager Chuck Tanner*

"The only time close counts is in horseshoes and dancing."

>—*Baseball manager Fred Haney*

"When you win, you eat better, you sleep better, and your wife looks like Gina Lollabridgida."

—*Baseball manager Johnny Pesky*

"Before you can win a game, you have to not lose it."

—*Football coach Chuck Noll*

"When we lost I couldn't sleep at night. When we win I can't sleep at night. But when you win, you wake up feeling better."

—*Baseball manager Joe Torre*

"Winning is the epitome of honesty itself."

—*Ohio State football coach Woody Hayes*

"Some coaches pray for wisdom. I pray for 260-pound tackles. They'll give me plenty of wisdom."

—*Pittsburgh Steelers football coach Chuck Noll*

WORK ETHIC

"Those who work the hardest are the last to surrender."

—*Basketball coach Rick Pitino*

"Hard work and togetherness. They go hand in hand. You need the hard work because it's such a tough atmosphere—to win week in and week out. You need togetherness because you don't always win, and you gotta hang tough together."

—*Football coach Tony Dungy*

"I don't like the subtle infiltration of 'something for nothing' philosophies into the very hearthstone of the American family. I believe that 'Thou shalt earn the bread by the sweat of thy face' was a benediction and not a penalty. Work is the zest of life; there is joy in its pursuit."

—*Baseball manager and general manager Branch Rickey*

UCLA

JOHN WOODEN

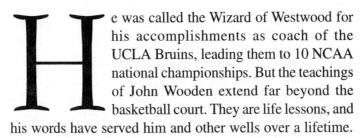

He was called the Wizard of Westwood for his accomplishments as coach of the UCLA Bruins, leading them to 10 NCAA national championships. But the teachings of John Wooden extend far beyond the basketball court. They are life lessons, and his words have served him and other wells over a lifetime.

Born on October 14, 1910, in Martinsville, Indiana, Wooden was a star basketball player at Martinsville High School, leading his team to a state championship in 1927 and to runner-up status two other years, in 1926 and 1928. The 5-foot 10-inch, 185-pound Wooden was all-state for all three of those seasons.

Wooden continued his basketball career at Purdue University, where he was a three-time All-American and led Purdue to the Big Ten Championship twice in 1930 and 1932, and the national championship in 1932 as well. He was team captain in 1931 and 1932, and was known as the "Indiana Rubber Man" for his suicidal dives on the court.

He began his illustrious coaching career immediately upon graduating from Purdue in 1932, coaching at Dayton High School in Dayton, Kentucky from 1932 to 1934 and Central High School in South Bend, Indiana, from 1934 to 1943. He had a remarkable record of 218-42 over that period.

Wooden moved on to the college ranks in 1946, and what is forgotten is that the first two years of his college coaching career he spent at Indiana State University (1946–1948). Of course, he was outstanding, posting a 47-14 record and leading Indiana State to the conference title in 1947 and the finals of the NAIA Invitational Tournament in 1948. Then he took the job that would make him the most successful coach in the history of college basketball: running the program at UCLA.

From 1948 to 1975, Wooden built a program that became the standard for excellence in college sports. Under Wooden, the Bruins won 19 PAC 10 championships, and 10 NCAA national titles, including seven straight championships from 1966 to 1973. They had four 30-0 seasons. He had one stretch where his teams won 88 straight games. During his tenure at UCLA, Wooden was named NCAA College Basketball Coach of the Year six times, and had a record of 620-147 and 885-203 overall, when he retired in 1975 after 40 years of coaching.

John Wooden is one of only two people enshrined in the Hall of Fame as a player and as a coach—the other is Lenny Wilkens. Wooden's basketball legacy is not just as a coach, but as a teacher as well. He coached a number of players who went on to become NBA greats, including Lew Alcindor (who changed his named to Kareem Abdul Jabbar), and Bill Walton, whose players, to this day, stay in close contact with Wooden, because he is still teaching them. If there was a Hall of Fame for words of wisdom, John Wooden would be there as well.

John Wooden on:

Ability

"Don't measure yourself by what you have accomplished, but by what you should have accomplished with your ability."

"Ability is a poor man's wealth."

"Ability may get you to the top, but it takes character to keep you there."

Achievement

"Don't mistake activity for achievement."

"You can't let praise or criticism get to you. It's a weakness to get caught up in either one."

Adversity

"Adversity is the state in which man mostly easily becomes acquainted with himself, being especially free of admirers then."

Attitude

"Things turn out best for the people who make the best of the way things turn out."

"The athlete who says that something cannot be done should never interrupt the one who is doing it."

BOOKS

"The worst thing about new books is that they keep us from reading the old ones."

BOSSES

"I think anyone in a position of supervision, if they're not listening to those under them, they're not going to get good results. The supervisor must make sure that all of those under his supervision understand they're working with him, not for him. I think if you work for someone, you punch the clock in and out and that's it. If you're working with someone, you want to do more than that."

CHAMPIONS

"I have often said, 'The mark of a true champion is to always perform near your own level of competency.'"

CHARACTER

"Winning takes talent, to repeat takes character."

"What you are as a person is far more important than what you are as a basketball player."

"Talent is God-given. Be humble. Fame is man-given. Be grateful. Conceit is self-given. Be careful."

"Be more concerned with your character than your reputation, because your character is what you really are, while your reputation is merely what others think you are."

"It isn't what you do, but how you do it."

COACHING

"A coach is someone who can give correction without causing resentment."

"Some of the greatest teaching jobs are being done by coaches that don't have very outstanding records, because they're not located in a situation where they have an opportunity to have an outstanding record. Yet they may be coming closer to getting the maximum potential out of what they have than somebody who is winning championships."

"We practiced by working hard on fundamentals, teaching fundamentals, imaginary jump-shooting and rebounding, change of pace drills, defensive sliding and things of that sort. Make each drill go quickly. Don't waste time between them. I believe that's better than having them run or do push-ups. I want the conditioning to come through fundamental drills. Don't waste time. I like to keep my practices not very long but very active. Don't stop playing to talk. Just keep going."

"Try to teach the best you can. For every player that makes good, there are far more who don't."

COURAGE

"Success is never final, failure is never fatal. It's courage that counts."

DESIRE

"I do not want players who do not have a keen desire to win and do not play hard and aggressively to accomplish that objective."

DISCIPLINE

"If you don't have time to do it right, when will you have time to do it over?"

"You cannot attain and maintain physical condition unless you are morally and mentally conditioned. And it is impossible to be in moral condition unless you are spiritually conditioned. I always told my players that our team condition depended on two factors: how hard they worked on the floor during practice and how well they behaved between practices."

"Discipline yourself, and others won't need to."

"If you lose self-control, everything will fall. You cannot function physically or mentally or in any other way unless your emotions are under control."

DISSENT

"If everybody agreed on everything, it would be a very dull, monotonous world."

EDUCATION

"It's what you learn after you know it all that counts."

EFFORT

"I continually stress to my players that all I expect from them at practice and in the games is their maximum effort."

FAILURE

"Failure is not fatal, but failure to change might be."

Faith

"There are many things that are essential to arriving at true peace of mind, and one of the most important is faith, which cannot be acquired without prayer."

"I never tried to determine the religion or the politics of an individual. I wanted to always stay open-minded, and I wanted them to have something in which they believed."

"For years now, I have carried a little cross in my pocket. Few people, except my immediate family, are aware of it at all. It was clutched in my hand during all of the games I coached."

Motivation

"I believe in not teaching through fear and I believed in keeping it as positive as you can. I never mentioned winning. You can't find a player who heard me mention winning."

"The best way to get anyone's attention is to show interest and listen to them. We don't learn anything except what we learn from others. If you show interest, I think they'll listen to you. It has to be consistent, not part-time."

"The best motivator is a pat on the back. All being different, sometimes the pat has to be lower."

"Praise is a great motivator. Criticism is a great teaching tool if done properly, but praise is the best motivator."

Perseverance

"Don't let what you cannot do interfere with what you can do."

"It's not so important who starts the game, but who finishes it."

"There's no great fun, satisfaction, or joy derived from doing something that's easy."

PERSPECTIVE

"Don't get engrossed over things you have no control or it will adversely affect the things you can control."

"I believe that for every artificial peak you create, you also create valleys. When you get too high for anything, emotion takes over and consistency of performance is lost and you will be unduly affected when adversity comes."

PLAYERS

"Good players can take coaching; great players can take coaching and learn."

PREPARATION

"It's the little details that are vital. Little things make big things happen."

"Rather than having my teams prepare to play a certain team each week, I prepared to play anybody. I didn't want my players worrying about the other fellows. I wanted them executing the sound offensive and defensive principles we taught in practice."

SELFLESSNESS

"You can't live a perfect day without doing something for someone who will never be able to repay you."

"Consider the rights of others before your own feelings, and the feelings of others before your own rights."

"Happiness begins where selfishness ends."

SPORTS

"Sports do not build character. They reveal it."

SUCCESS

"Success is peace of mind, which is a direct result of self-satisfaction in knowing you did your best to become the best that you are capable of becoming."

TAUNTING

"I wanted talking, but I never wanted any taunting. I see entirely too much of that today, and I think coaches can stop that if they wanted to. If I caught a player doing it, I certainly would not let it go unnoticed—he'd hear from me."

TEAMWORK

"I never permitted a player to criticize a teammate. I wouldn't permit that. I also insisted that a player never score without acknowledging somebody else."

WINNING

"Although I wanted my players to work to win, I tried to convince them they had always won when they had done their best."

WORK ETHIC

"Nothing will work unless you do."

"Earn the right to be proud and confident."

YOUTH

"Young people need models, not critics."

•••

JOHN WOODEN'S NINE PROMISES THAT CAN BRING HAPPINESS:

- "Promise yourself that you will talk health, happiness, and prosperity as often as possible."
- "Promise yourself to make all your friends know there is something in them that is special and that you value."
- "Promise to think only of the best, to work only for the best, and to expect only the best in yourself and others."
- "Promise to be just as enthusiastic about the success of others as you are about your own."
- "Promise yourself to be so strong that nothing can disturb your peace of mind."
- "Promise to forget the mistakes of the past and press on to greater achievements in the future."
- "Promise to wear a cheerful appearance at all times and give every person you meet a smile."
- "Promise to give so much time to improving yourself that you have no time to criticize others."
- "Promise to be too large for worry, too noble for anger, too strong for fear, and too happy to permit trouble to press on you."

ABOUT THE AUTHOR

Thom Loverro is a sports columnist for *The Washington Times*. The winner of numerous writing awards, Loverro joined *The Baltimore Sun* in 1984 as a reporter and editor. In 1992, he moved to the *Times*, where he has covered the Washington Redskins, Baltimore Orioles, and a host of other sports, including several Olympics. He also teaches journalism at American University in Washington, D.C. Loverro lives in Columbia, Maryland, with his wife Liz, and two sons, Rocco and Nick.

Thom Loverro's previous books include *The Washington Redskins, The Authorized History* (1996); *Home of the Game: the Story of Camden Yards* (1999); and *Cammi Granato, Hockey Pioneer* (2000).